Knits from a Painter's Palette

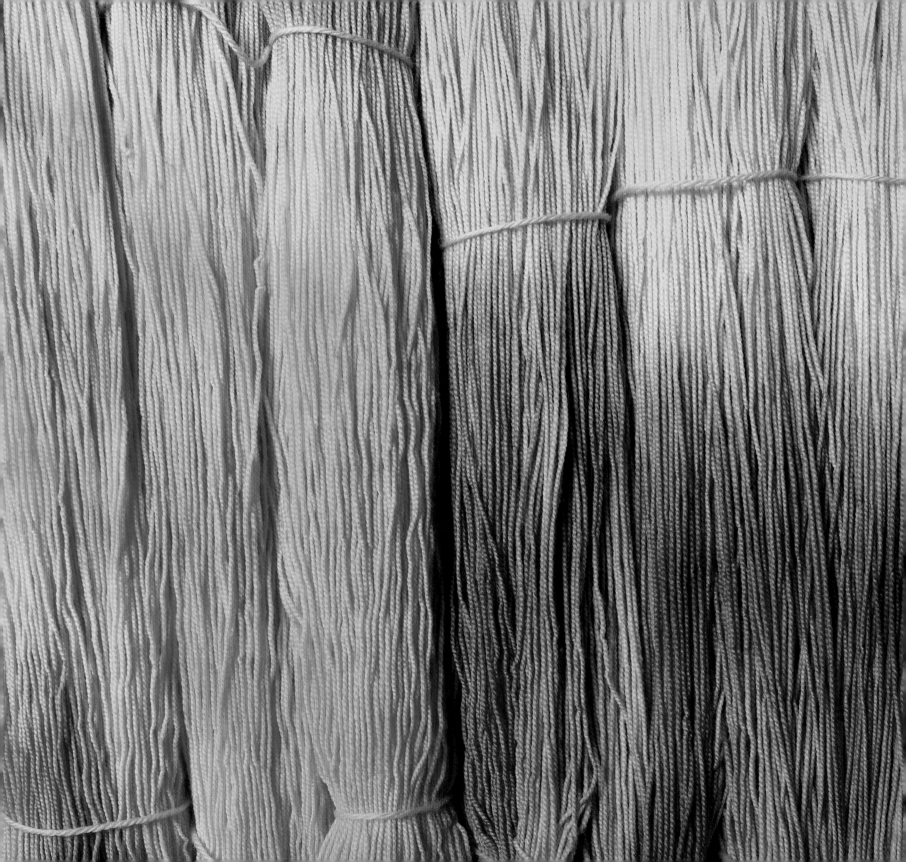

Knits from a **Painter's Palette**

Modular Masterpieces in Handpainted Yarns

Maie Landra

Koigu Wool Designs

sixth&springbooks

Sixth&Spring Books
233 Spring St
New York, NY 10013

Vice President, Publisher
TRISHA MALCOLM

Editorial Director
ELAINE SILVERSTEIN

Art Director
CHI LING MOY

Graphic Designer
SHEENA T. PAUL

Book Division Manager
ERICA SMITH

Associate Editor
ERIN WALSH

Instructions Editors
ROSEMARY DRYSDALE
SHIRI MOR
CARLA SCOTT

Essay
SHIRLEY SCOTT

Instructions Proofreader
MARY LOU EASTMAN

Fashion Stylist
ZEINA ESMAIL

Hair & Makeup
SHAWNA BOWEN

Production Manager
DAVID JOINNIDES

Photography
MOOISHI
DAN HOWELL

President, Sixth&Spring Books
ART JOINNIDES

Library of Congress Control Number: 2006924831

ISBN: 1-933027-06-1

ISBN 13: 978-1-933027-06-7

1 3 5 7 9 10 8 6 4 2

Manufactured in China

First Edition

Contents

◆ Modular Knitting

Dedication

To my grandchildren, Lisanne, Karling, Kersti, and Rishi

Introduction

KOIGU™ WOOL DESIGNS is generally known to the consumer as Koigu. Koigu represents color, a multitude of colors. Since all the variegated yarns are originals, each knitter who knits one of our designs will have a true one-of-a-kind.

This book is a celebration of Koigu Painter's Palette Premium Merino (KPPPM). Recently, a consumer stated that KPPPM is like truffles— rare and quickly snatched up when found.

The long journey to the Koigu of today has been exciting and full of discoveries for us. It has been a true evolution, from our early days spinning fleece and experiencing different wool fibers to dyeing, knitting and weaving the yarns. A combination of positive happenings has eventually led to positive results.

Hand-painting KPPPM is our way of experiencing the emotions we receive from the world, people, art, and music, and at the same time keeping our minds free of preconceptions. We speak through color; design is the tool we use to translate that color.

This book features both patterns for the novice and challenges for the advanced knitter. You will discover that Koigu patterns take you to another dimension in design and color. I encourage you to explore variegated yarns in your own way and according to your own taste.

Be inspired!

Maie Landra

The World of Koigu

Where is the world of Koigu, and what will you
find there? The name "Koigu" is enigmatic and
intriguing, suggesting a fantastic kingdom of
the imagination, a distant realm in Japan, or
perhaps an exotic breed of the finest sheep.
You wouldn't be wrong in thinking these
things, because Koigu does not appear on any
ordinary map. It is the farm and business of
Maie Landra, her daughter Taiu, and her young
granddaughter Kersti; the name chosen to
honor the ancestral home of Maie's late
husband Harry in their native Estonia. On the
family's land is a vintage farmhouse and barn, a
long wool shed, a serpentine pond, and beauty
as far as the eye can see. And that's only on the
outside. Inside is a world of color and the joy it
brings. It is also a world of talent, a world of
family, and a world of hard work.

For more than a decade, Koigu Wool Designs has supplied top-quality handpainted merino yarn and exquisite knitting designs to consumers across North America. Its unique, rich palette, as glorious as a painter's, has ignited a passion for color and quality in the knitting world. How is it that such vibrant energy emanates from this quiet, secluded farm?

The creative spirit often flourishes in peaceful surroundings, and that is exactly what happened to Maie and Taiu Landra—two exceptional women who have fashioned a whole life from their musings, experiments and discoveries with color and design. This is their story.

Above: Leaving Germany to Canada 1948, Maie in the knit hat from Estonia Opposite: Watercolor exhibit, 1960

A Portrait of an Artist

As a consequence of the upheavals of World War II, Maie's family fled Estonia when she was a small child. After their escape, they spent several years in a displaced persons camp in the American zone in Germany. There were many children of a similar age in the camp, and parents made great efforts to make sure their days were as happy and unscarred as possible. Birthdays were always remembered with ceremony. Maie recalls her mother knitting a sweater for a German woman in exchange for enough sugar to make her a birthday cake.

The family was eventually sponsored to come to Canada, where they lived and worked on a flower seed farm on Vancouver Island. From even these very early days, Maie remembers how her mother beautified their lives in a strange new country. The colors of the flowers on the farm were endless. On walks together, mother and daughter would admire the richly colored velvet petals and the faces on each pansy. Maie's mother, a highly skilled weaver and weaving teacher, managed to acquire a loom from a Finnish family. Since there was no weaving yarn available on the Island, she ordered the yarn by mail. Appalled by the crude colors of yarn that arrived, she set about over-dyeing them with simple dime store dyes, the only ones that were readily available. Maie often assisted. At the age of 10, she undertook the sophisticated task of enlarging and charting traditional Estonian knitting and weaving designs taken from tiny photographs in her mother's treasures. Even at this early age, Maie was receiving subliminal training in the particulars of textile work. Her life was steeped in cultural tradition, and she had begun to internalize Estonian design.

When the opportunity presented itself, the family moved to Toronto to be a part of its active Estonian community. During her days at school, Maie was encouraged to fill any spare moments with drawing and painting. Recognition came early; one teacher even asked permission to keep some of her work for his personal collection. After high school, Maie entered the Ontario College of Art, from which she graduated in 1960 with a degree in drawing and painting. She spent her college

years exploring all facets of art, but her favorite mediums were watercolor and egg tempura. Today, many of the pieces she created during that time still fill her home.

Maie, prepared to be a visual artist, never dreamed she would find her calling in the world of textiles. Even in those days, however, fashion was hugely important in her life. Before today's anything-goes casual living, dressing well was an art that played an especially important role in the social life of the time. Maie and her mother always designed and made their own clothes, sometimes ornamenting them with traditional motifs, embroideries and surface design. No two outfits were ever alike. These clothes were so well-made that some of them are still in Maie's wardrobe today. Although they are now brought out more to admire than to wear, Maie's two daughters always had plenty to choose from when periods of retro dressing came into vogue over the years.

Maie, true to herself and unwilling to ignore her calling, continued to work as a professional artist even after marrying Harry. She frequently exhibited her work both independently and

The Koigu Wool Farm

In 1972, when the children were young, Maie and Harry bought a large farm a few hours' drive from Toronto to use as a weekend retreat. Ten years later, Maie finally came to the realization that in order to truly explore wool, fiber, spinning and dyeing yarn for the tapestries she was creating, she must live in this peaceful country place year-round. This would mean raising sheep for wool—something Maie admits to knowing next to nothing about at the time. Family and friends greeted this announcement with every emotion, from dismay and disbelief to sheer derision. Undeterred, the Landras made the move to the farm.

They all had a lot to learn. Maie, finding herself excited by the huge variety of natural colors in the family's new flock of sheep, began to spin fleeces, often including her own hand-dyed fibers in her handspun yarn. Although her original intention was to use the homegrown wool in her tapestries, her focus quickly changed. She found that knitting a sweater from the newly created yarn became a faster way of seeing the end result than making an entire tapestry.

with artist groups, always sandwiching her art between the responsibilities of maintaining a home and raising her three children, Karl, Karin and Taiu. Knitting for the children was also a must. Maie's house became filled with handmade textiles that she wove under the instruction of her mother. Weaving grew into a passion for Maie, but she was forever frustrated with the limited color selection of yarns available in stores.

Taiu, then a young teenager, embraced farm life from the very beginning. She learned to spin and knit sweaters and joined the 4-H Club and other youth leadership organizations, often exhibiting her family's sheep at agricultural fairs. Eventually, she went on to attend the Ontario Agricultural College to study business. Although the Landras had tried everything from selling freezer lamb to tanning hides to turn a profit from their sheep, the business was still being subsidized by Harry's law practice. Not surprisingly, Taiu's main focus after graduation was to find a way to make raising sheep and wool economically viable.

As Maie and Taiu shared the farm work and managed business details together, their mother-daughter bond grew strong. While Taiu experimented with developing her own sweater designs, kits and original garments, Maie concentrated on making one-of-a-kind wearable art from handspun wool that had been beautifully dyed by hand. Since hand-spinning took a huge amount of time, the women investigated shipping their wool clip to outside woolen mills for processing. They also worked conscientiously to improve the quality of their homegrown fleece through breeding programs. Gradually, as a result of customer demand, they began to explore broader knitwear markets, drafting their own patterns and selling knitting kits and sweaters at craft shows. Customers on the craft show circuit weren't shy about speaking their minds, and many made suggestions for a lighter merino wool that could be worn indoors—one that could be worn close to the skin. Maie and Taiu listened, and by the late 1990s, the satisfaction and rewards they had been striving for were finally starting to be realized.

Opposite page: Koigu sheep on the farm

Left: Taiu showing sheep at the local fair, 1986

A Yarn is Born: The Development of KPPPM

One auspicious day, a summer resident who spent his vacations near the Koigu farm happened to call the Landra household. Although he called about something unrelated, it came up in conversation that the man was a retired industrialist who had once operated a huge commercial woolen mill. He was still well-connected in the field, and he knew where fine merino wool could be spun to specifications. Maie and Taiu recognized the opportunity, and that summer, Koigu Painter's Palette Premium Merino—or KPPPM, as it is affectionately known—was conceived.

Although KPPPM was unlike any other yarn on the market, Maie and Taiu still had some high hurdles to clear to get their new product off the ground. The wool had to be paid for in cash, up front, and the initial minimum quantity seemed huge. An advertisement in Vogue Knitting magazine produced a deluge of responses, however, and suddenly the family was doing business on a scale they had never dreamed of.

Dyeing the yarn was filled with challenges and discoveries as well. Each skein was an adventure. Maie approached handpainting yarn the same way she approached painting her watercolors, and although it might have seemed like she was working largely from intuition, her formal art training undoubtedly played a part in her experimentations. When customers began requesting specific colorways, Maie and Taiu knew they needed to devise a way to record their creations. A dye book emerged: a slim, blue volume as tattered and stained as a chef's cookbook, with notes beginning at the back of the book instead of the front. No outside observer could decipher it, let alone copy its secrets, but it is the system the women continue to use to this day.

The Koigu sense of mission developed gradually and intuitively. Maie and Taiu would produce fine merino knitting yarn that could be worn next to the skin. They would paint it by hand in small batches. Each individual skein would be a painter's palette in itself. Where some designers might use a dozen colors in a single sweater, Maie would use a dozen in a single skein. The complete range of colorways would give the knitting world choices that had never before been imagined.

But would such a yarn sell? It was a very big question. One concern was that the gauge was too fine; common wisdom of the time said that knitters wanted only heavy weights of yarn that would produce faster results. Another concern was that since KPPPM was such a visual yarn, people might not be willing to buy it by mail. Both, however, proved to be unfounded. "KPPPM became one of the best-selling and least-returned yarns at Patternworks, defying rational understanding," explains Linda Skolnik, founder of the successful catalog mail-order business and author of The Knitting Way. "Each skein is simply a handpainted work of art." The Koigu Wool Designs identity had been born.

For the first five years, KPPPM was produced in a laundry tub that had been installed in the farmhouse kitchen. The Landras wore out two brand new ceramic-topped stoves before they realized that buying secondhand stoves was a better idea. In the evenings, Maie and Taiu reeled the yarn into 50-gram skeins by hand. Harry wrote yarn labels in his spare time.

In good weather, the wool was hung to dry outside on the pine trees; in the winter, it was hung over the bathtub. The living room, constantly filled with crates of wool, was used as a showroom for customers. The family soon realized that if the business was to grow, a larger workspace was essential to meet customer demand. Construction on a wool shed began in 1999, and the transition from retail to wholesale business followed.

Opposite page:
the Koigu barn
Left: Drying yarn
on the pine tree

Making Koigu Magic: Producing KPPPM Today

These days, the Landra farmhouse is used only for eating and sleeping; it is the wool shed where the Koigu heart beats strongest. At more than 4,500 square feet, the shed is an impressive building with a warehouse and showroom as well as separate areas for dyeing and drying the wool, reeling it into skeins, and shipping it off. Maie finally has the studio of her dreams; Taiu, who has temporarily put her own design career on hold to take on the responsibility of turning the family's art into a viable business, now has a large office; and granddaughter Kersti has a playroom. Kersti has grown up in the wool shed. Her playpen was stationed there permanently when she was a baby, and she now likes to play basketball in the warehouse area.

The process of creating Koigu wool is both physical and highly personal. The Landras use machines to assist them wherever possible, but

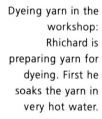

Dyeing yarn in the workshop: Rhichard is preparing yarn for dyeing. First he soaks the yarn in very hot water.

handpainting yarn is a true artisan process. The quantities for each dye lot are very small. The work depends to a huge degree on the sensitivity of the dyer, not on the meticulous following of recipes. Stippling and other sophisticated techniques require a great deal of control, training and practice. The entire Koigu workforce consists only of the Landras and a small handful of local employees; of these people, only Maie, Taiu, and Rhichard Devrieze, a fellow fiber artist, are able to dye and paint the yarn. It took Rhichard three years apprenticing under Maie to learn how to handpaint in the spirit of Koigu—and he admits that he still has more to learn. Only Maie herself can dye one entire range of colors, and for this she still uses an improbable-looking batterie de cuisine consisting of old, stained measuring cups and tiny spoons.

Many factors can influence the outcome of the dyelots. The individual personality, mood, feelings and thoughts of the artist all have an impact. The environment also plays a part—the Landras and Rhichard continue to be surprised

Skeins are hung to dry in the heated drying room under special drying conditions. A large fan is used to make sure there is good air circulation.

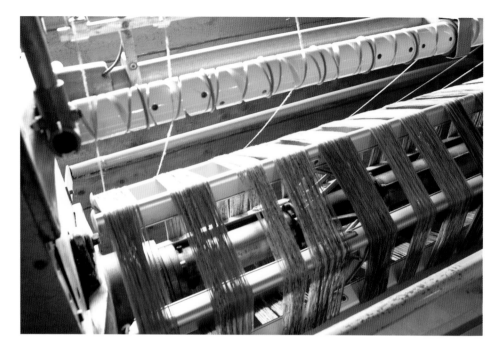

at the effect that even weather conditions have on each batch of dyed yarn. Maie has been quoted as saying that the perfect dyelot must be alive with highlights and depth, not dead and lifeless, and a refreshing aspect of KPPPM is indeed that it is fearless, bold and luminous, with a spark of life in each dyelot. No two dyelots are exactly the same.

As Koigu devotees know, KPPPM colorways are not named but numbered, following the

Above and right: Machines are used to measure, wind and cut skeins into portions that are ready to be twisted.

method of the great musical composers who assigned a number to each work within an opus. Knitters have become accustomed to this system, and the Landras have now created more than 300 colorways, each one a palette in itself.

Where do these colorways come from? They come from every hue of forest and field, every flower and fruit, and every sunset and sunrise, from all the world's skies and oceans in their many moods, and from every nuance of every season. Maie has developed most of them, although Kersti, an artistic child, has created five of her own. There are no color charts on the walls of the wool shed or painting treatises on the bookshelves—the colors spring spontaneously from Maie's fertile brain, though she is doubtlessly influenced by the world around her and her early formal training. Taiu has noticed that some of her mother's yarn palettes are the same as those found in her earlier paintings, resonating throughout her artistic career.

Left: Colorways are numbered, not named. Numbers are written on the blackboard to keep track of favorite colorways.

The Koigu Mystique: Maie Landra's Design World

There is drama in a Maie Landra original design. The styling is fashion-forward and sophisticated, belying its earthy country origins, and the garments are always thrilling both to make and to wear. Even those knit in subtle, understated colorways boast fine shaping and attractive stitch work, making it impossible for the wearer of a Koigu garment to ever hide in the back row of the chorus.

Maie's first instinct as a designer is to clothe the whole body—to create a complete presentation, not merely to accessorize. Although she has designed dozens of quick-knit take-along projects in response to knitting trends, her greatest work and greatest love is the knitted ensemble. Dresses, long skirts with matching jackets, even women's pants—that territory where most knitwear designers fear to tread—have been the focus of her bold adventuring. The amount of work and yarn needed to make a Landra ensemble may seem daunting, but it deters neither the designer nor her many devotees. To the contrary, Koigu knitters often describe feeling a sense of loss when the work is done, some even claiming they can't bear to put the finishing touches on a garment.

The design process can be as much a form of alchemy as the dyeing process, but if there is a single passion that rules Maie's design sense, it is the combining of variegated yarns. She loves to make swatches—to simply select from a basket of yarns, and to note how colors change their personality when combined with other colors. Sometimes these swatches grow into important projects, such as the Spirit Skirt that sparked Maie's ongoing exploration of the hexagonal form. Other times a swatch will simply lie on the back of the sofa until it reveals its own destiny, as with the now-famous Oriental Jacket. Mother and daughter are highly in tune in matters of taste, and sometimes the swatches speak to Taiu first. Her role in critiquing Maie's work is very important to Koigu Wool Designs, and both women must agree on each project if it is to move forward.

Sometimes Maie gives herself a specific technical challenge while designing. The Keepsake Shawl, for example, began as an exploration of what could be made from a

Opposite page:
Groovy dress
and shawl

Left: Mother and
daughter in hand-
spun jackets

single large mitered square. Developing a beautiful garment from a forbidden technique also ignites her creativity—a "no-no" in the knitting world is to her a challenge, a new problem to solve. The usual wisdom among knitting experts, for example, is that lace and variegated yarns simply do not mix. In the Charlotte's Web Shawl, however, Maie develops this combination into high art, featuring lace in five different variegates.

Modular Knitting: Maie's Muse

When Maie began to experiment with combining variegated yarn and modular segments, she stepped into a brave new world of design possibilities. Although she still employs a variety of techniques in her designs, it her spectacular modular knitting—the focus of this book—that Koigu is perhaps best known for. Maie loves manipulating geometric shapes, from squares and triangles to cubes and chevrons. She is particularly captivated by hexagons, a fascination that began when she wondered what would happen if she made the double decreases characteristic of modular knitting on every row instead of only on alternate rows. She tried it, and a little pie-shaped wedge came into being. Next, she became intrigued with varying the colors within the motif itself. Then she couldn't resist picking up stitches on the selvage until the circle was complete. And, eventually, what began as a simple idea sketched on a tiny scrap of paper grew into the Spirit Skirt. In Maie's world, you can plan as much as you want, but the surprises and discoveries—and the designs they spark—are often intuitive.

Koigu Style:
Signature Techniques

Flattering lines, an elegant drape and crisp finishing characterize a Koigu original, and Maie consciously designs to flatter many figure types. Line can be as important as color in Koigu fashion. In some modular projects, the lines formed by the decreases in continuous segments point downward, adding unattractive gravitational pull to the body. In contrast, Koigu Wool Designs' Jeans Vest, with its upward decrease lines, shows how slimming modular knitting can be in the hands of an attentive expert. In this and other earlier works, Maie even accepted the challenge of knitting pants and jackets to the female form. Modular Knitting is described and illustrated on pp 28–33.

The drape of shawls and skirts is not haphazard in Koigu style, and different methods are used to ensure that shawls float over the shoulders and scarves flatter necks with their softness. Maie sometimes plays with the notion of using drop stitch and other openwork patterns to create this drape, as in the Floppy Jacket.

Alternatively, the flaring skirt in Midnight Rapture is the result of careful control over gauge, changing needle sizes rather than incorporating decreases into the shaping. You'll find strong, crisp borders in Maie's work, often achieved by using a crochet stitch to add firmness to edges and to fine-tune the fit. Her necklines do not stretch, and she sometimes adds a couture touch by incorporating knitted facings where needed. The strips that form the Groovy Dress are joined with Maie's signature version of the three-needle bind off, worked with a crochet hook and in a contrasting color.

As with all hand-knits, blocking to size is very important. An unblocked shawl or skirt looks shriveled and unpromising, while blocking sets the stitch and gives a professional finish. Maie soaks her work in warm water, then pins the garment to size. (If the garment has openwork stitches, she stretches it to maximum size before pinning.)

Because KPPPM responds beautifully to the finest finishing treatments, knitters have the chance to create a truly custom garment.

Experience the Color: The Koigu Challenge

The patterns in this book are accessible to all. You'll find a feast of techniques, from simple knit and purl patterns that take on new life, to the stunning effects of advanced modular knitting. Color choice is personal; there are no set rules for combining solid or variegated KPPPM colors. The best way to choose color combinations is to simply trust your own instincts. Don't be afraid of color—allow it to speak to you. A safe way to choose colors that will work well together is to find a common color among your selection of variegated yarns. For example, try combining pinks with touches of purples, purples with touches of pink, blues with highlights of pink, and so on. Follow our suggestions, or choose colors and projects to please the artist within you.

Since the launch of Koigu Painter's Palette Premium Merino, thousands of knitters have taken the Koigu challenge and produced their own wearable art. KPPPM has been used to fashion everything from baby booties to burial clothes, elaborate tapestries to the embroidery on slippers, Indian shawls to ancient German fishing flies. Some people even claim that the yarn has Zen power. Knitters and non-knitters alike are happy to simply contemplate the delicacies of each skein—its interplay of color and the mood it creates—and to pay tribute to its effect on the human spirit.

Stitch Workshop

Modular knitting, mitered squares, patchwork, domino knitting—whatever you choose to call it, this technique opens up endless possibilities for knitters. And once you've mastered the basics, you'll find it highly addictive—especially when you're working with hand-dyed yarns. The way the colors and stitches interact will mesmerize you, making it practically impossible to stop.

The principle behind modular knitting is simple—a geometric shape is formed with a series of decreases; shapes can be constructed in various ways to form diamonds, triangles or rectangles. To create adjacent pieces, stitches are picked up along a side of the previous shape and extended by casting on additional stitches.

Make a Practice Square before making any modular garment. Then add on to your square to learn how to knit the square together. You will need to know these two cast-on techniques for the Practice Square.

Knit-on Cast On (K-cast on)

(Used when casting on at the beg of a row.) Make slip knot on LH needle. With 2nd needle knit into slip knot loop and place new stitch onto LH needle. *K in between first 2 sts on LH needle and place new stitch onto LH needle. Work stitch through back of loop (tbl). Rep from * to desired number sts on LH needle.

Loop Cast On (L-cast on)

(Used when casting on at the end of a row.) Make slip knot on LH needle. Cont making loops on needle to desired number of sts.

PRACTICE SQUARE

Cast on 25 sts using the K-cast on.
Row 1 (WS) K24 tbl, p1.
Row 2 Sl 1 knitwise, k10 tbl, SK2P (sl 1, k2tog, psso), k10 tbl, p1.
Row 3 Sl 1, k tbl to last st, p1.
Row 4 Sl 1, k9 tbl, SK2P, k9 tbl, p1.
Rep rows 3 and 4, decreasing 2 sts at center every RS row and working 1 less st either side of dec every dec row, until 3 sts rem, ending with a RS row.

Last row (WS) Sl 1, p2tog, psso. Keep the rem st open to be knit later.

Knitting squares together vertically

To make Square B, pick up remaining st from Square A. Turn. With RS facing, pick up and k 11 sts along upper edge of A, pick up and k 1 st in cast-on loop at left corner of A (13 sts). Turn. With WS facing, K-cast on 12 sts (25 sts). Beginning with row 1, work instructions as for Square A. Work Square C same as Square B.

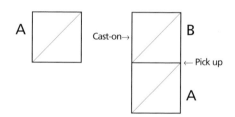

Knitting squares together horizontally

To make Square D, k-cast on 12 sts. Holding Squares A, B and C, with RS facing k1 in cast-on loop at lower right-hand corner of A. Pick up and k 11 sts along right side of A and 1 st from upper corner of A (25 sts). Beginning with row 1, work instructions as for Square A.

To make Square E, begin with 1 remaining st from Square D. Pick up and k 11 sts from upper edge of D, 1 st from upper corner of A, 11 sts from right side of B and 1 st from upper corner of B (25 sts). Beginning with row 1, work instructions as for Square A. Repeat for Square F.

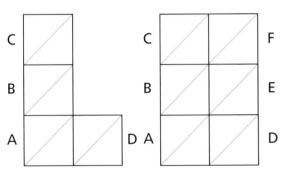

TRIANGLES

Right Angle Triangle

Cast on 13 sts using the K-cast on.

Row 1 (WS) K12 tbl, p1.

Row 2 Sl 1 knitwise, k9, k2tog, p1.

Row 3 Sl 1, k tbl to last st, p1.

Rep rows 2 and 3, decreasing 1 st every RS row, until 3 sts rem, ending with RS row.

Last row (WS) Sl 1, p2tog, psso. Keep the rem st open to be knit later.

Right angle triangle

Left Angle Triangle

Cast on 13 sts using the K-cast on.

Row 1 (WS) K12 tbl, p1.

Row 2 Sl 1 knitwise, sl1-k1-psso, k tbl to last st, p1.

Row 3 Sl 1, k tbl to last st, p1.

Rep rows 2 and 3, decreasing 1 st every RS row, until 3 sts rem, ending with RS row.

Last row (WS) Sl 1, p2tog, psso. Keep the rem st open to be knit later.

Left angle triangle

Half Square

Pick up 25 sts along sides of two squares, 13 sts along one side of one square and 12 sts along one side of other square.

Row 1 (WS) K to last st, p1.

Row 2 Sl 1, k2tog, k8 tbl, sl 1-k2tog-psso, k8 tbl, k2tog, p1.

Row 3 Sl 1, k19 tbl, p1.

Row 4 Sl 1, k2tog, k6 tbl, sl 1-k2tog-psso, k6 tbl, k2tog, p1.

Row 5 Sl 1, k15 tbl, p1.

Row 6 Sl 1, k2tog, k4 tbl, sl 1-k2tog-psso, k4 tbl, k2tog, p1.

Row 7 Sl 1, k11 tbl, p1.

Row 8 Sl 1, k2tog, k2 tbl, sl 1-k2tog-psso, k2 tbl, k2tog, p1.

Row 9 Sl 1, k7 tbl, p1.

Row 10 Sl 1, k2tog, sl 1-k2tog-psso, k2tog, p1.

Row 11 Sl1, k3 tbl, p1.

Draw the yarn through the 5 rem sts and pull tog.

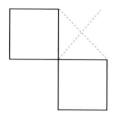

DIAMOND

In the diamond shape, work the decreases from the four corners to the center (see diagram.)

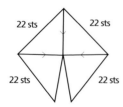

22 sts   22 sts

22 sts   22 sts

Cast on 88 st.

Row 1 (WS) Sl1, k to last st, p1.

Row 2 Sl1, k20, place marker, k2tog, k20, place marker, k2tog, k20, place marker, k2tog, k20, p1.

Repeat rows 1 and 2, working decreases as established on every RS row, until 7 sts rem. Cut yarn, draw through the 7 sts and pull together. Sew or use 3-needle join to close the open side of the diamond.

CHANGING THE DIRECTION OF DECREASES IN ADJOINING SHAPES

Decrease Changing from Up to Down

Pick up 13 sts along right side of square A. Cast on 12 additional stitches. Work Square B with decreases slanting down toward bottom right.

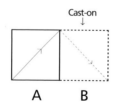

Cast-on
↓

A   B

Decrease Changing from Down to Up

Pick up 13 st along left side of square A. Cast on 12 additional stitches. Work Square B with decreases slanting up toward top left.

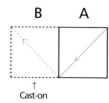

B   A

↑
Cast-on

Notes

1 Read carefully through instructions before beginning to knit.

2 Always work the knit sts through the back loop (tbl). Work the purl sts in the normal way.

3 Always pick up and k sts through the back loop and from the RS of the work.

4 Slip first st and p last st of every row for selvage sts.

5 Front and back are worked exactly the same.

6 When picking up sts along an edge, always pick up from the RS. This represents the first row of the pattern. The following row will be a WS row and row 2 of the pattern.

7 For ease in working, place markers to indicate the placement of the decs and sl these markers every row.

8 Work all decreases on the RS.

9 When changing color within a shape, begin the new color on the RS.

10 Always follow the direction of the decreases, as shown on the chart. Knit each piece to the shape and size down.

11 Join pieces with 2 needles and a crochet hook, as shown on p.33, rather than by sewing.

12 Weave in ends while working whenever possible.

CASTING ON the loop cast on and the knit-on cast on

Pick up stitches, then cast on at the end of a row using loop cast-on. Wrap yarn around left thumb from front to back. Insert needle through strand and slip loop onto needle.

The knit-on method is for the beginning of a row before picking up stitches. Make a slip knot, knit next st and place new loop onto needle. Continue for desired number of stitches.

K-TBL knitting through the back loop

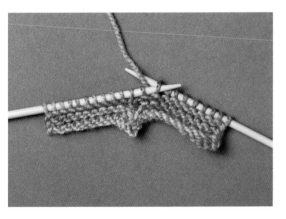

To make the shapes appear neater, always knit all knit stitches through the back loop as shown. This twists them and makes a firmer fabric.

The garter-stitch square on the left was knit in the front loop, while the square on the right was knit in the back loop. Knitting in the back loop creates more defined stitches.

Again, the left seed-stitch square was knit in the front loop and the right in the back loop. **Note:** Always work purl stitches in the normal way.

SHAPE UP squares, triangles, diamonds

When working a square of two different colors, work the center decrease as follows: slip 1 with color 1, knit 2 together with color 2, then psso.

To join a right-angle triangle to a left-angle triangle, on a RS row, work to the last st and slip to RH needle, pick up 1 st at side of left triangle and k it tog with the last st.

Working decreases at both ends and in the center creates a half-square. When 5 stitches remain, draw the yarn through all sts and pull tog.

Another version of a half-square is created by casting on an odd number of stitches, then decreasing on each side until one stitch remains.

A diamond is constructed by decreasing from corners toward the center.

PICKING UP making multiple shapes

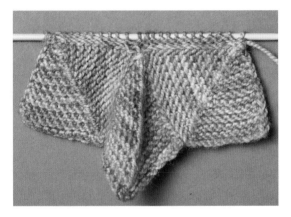

When picking up stitches, always insert the needle into the back loop of the stitch or row to create a ridge. Wrap yarn knitwise and pull through to complete the knit stitch.

When inserting a square into a 3-sided section, pick up and knit stitches along 2 sides, and at the end of the right-side rows, pick up a stitch along the third side and knit it together with the last stitch of the row.

SEAMING joining seams with two needles and a hook

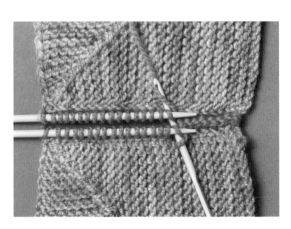

Pick up stitches (tbl) along the sides of each piece, then knit one row (tbl) with dpn's. To join the seam, with a crochet hook, *insert the hook into the first stitch on both needles and pull the yarn through both sts, drop sts from needles, yo hook and draw through two loops on hook.

Charlotte's Web Shawl

intermediate

Maie began to knit this shawl in a simple lace pattern, interchanging the colorways. The pattern is now legendary among knitters. The shawl uses five different variegated colorways, each one eased into the next. You may decide to knit some colorways wider than others. There are many choices.

FINISHED MEASUREMENTS

- Width 56"/142cm before blocking, 76"/193cm after blocking
- Length 24"/61cm before blocking, 38"/96cm after blocking

MATERIALS

- 1 1.75oz/50g skein of Koigu *Painter's Palette Premium Merino* (100% wool), 175yd/161m in each P319L, P117, P314L, P105L, P605
- Size US 6 (4mm) circular needle (used as straight needles), 32"/81cm long OR SIZE TO OBTAIN GAUGE
- Size E/4 (3.5mm) crochet hook

GAUGE

16 stitches and 28 rows = 4" (10cm) in lace pattern (after blocking).

TAKE TIME TO CHECK GAUGE.

LACE PATTERN

(multiple of 8 sts plus 1)

Row 1 (RS) *K2, yo, SKP, k1, k2tog, yo, k1; rep from * to last st, k1.

Rows 2, 4, 6, and 8 (WS) Purl.

Row 3 *K1, yo, SKP, yo, SK2P, yo, k2tog, yo; rep from * to last st, k1.

Row 5 *K1, yo, SK2P, yo, k1, yo, SK2P, yo; rep from * to last st, k1.

Row 7 *K1, yo, SK2P, yo, k1, yo, SK2P, yo; rep from * to last st, k1.

SHAWL

Cast on 7 stitches. This is the center of the long edge of the shawl.

Work 2 rows in stockinette stitch.

From here follow the chart, working in lace pattern and increasing as shown.

Note Only the odd-numbered (RS) rows are shown on chart. The shawl has a total of 154 rows. The chart shows the first 41 rows only. Work the WS rows as purl. The rows will naturally appear "broken" on the shawl, due to center increases. Continue in pattern established by chart, striping shawl as follows:

- Work 26 rows in P319L (including 2 stockinette stitch rows at beginning)
- 16 rows alternating P117 and P319L (2 rows in each)
- 16 rows in P117
- 16 rows alternating P314L and P117 (2 rows in each)
- 16 rows in P314L
- 16 rows alternating P105L and P314L (2 rows in each)
- 16 rows in P105L

◆ 16 rows alternating P605 and P105L (2 rows
  in each)
◆ 16 rows in P605
Bind off all stitches loosely.

Work 1 row in sc around entire shawl with
desired color.
Work the following 2 rows across bottom edge
(or bound-off edge) only:
Row 1 *Ch 9, skip 4 sc, sc into next sc;
rep from * across row, turn.

Row 2 *Ch 9, sc into next space;
rep from * across row.

Soak shawl in warm water and pin to
maximum size. Allow to dry.

Fringes are 5 halved 16"/40.5cm strands.
Mix colors, and attach at each crocheted loop
of bottom edge. ◆

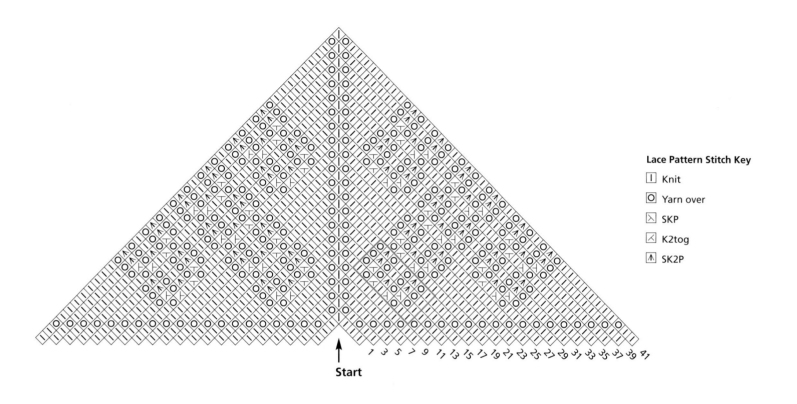

Start

Lace Pattern Stitch Key

| | Knit

| O | Yarn over

| ⊠ | SKP

| ⊠ | K2tog

| ⩑ | SK2P

Pillow

FINISHED MEASUREMENTS

◆ 13" x 13"/33cm x 33cm

MATERIALS

◆ 1 1.75oz/50g skein of Koigu *Painter's Palette Premium Merino* (100% wool), 175yd/161m in each P105L, P121L, and P812
◆ Size US 3 (3.25mm) needles OR SIZE TO OBTAIN GAUGE
◆ Size D/3 (3mm) crochet hook, or size to correspond with needle
◆ 13"/33cm square pillow form
◆ Stitch markers

GAUGE

28 stitches and 36 rows = 4" (10cm) in stockinette stitch.
TAKE TIME TO CHECK GAUGE.

TECHNIQUES

See Stitch Workshop for:

◆ Practice square
◆ Diamonds
◆ Triangles
◆ Joining seams with 2 needles and a crochet hook

Daydreams Pillow and Stroller Blanket
intermediate

This is an elegant blanket for a baby stroller, with a pillow to match. The softness of the yarn makes both perfect for a baby.

1st Side

SQUARE PATTERN

Each square uses 2 colors. Begin with color A, then switch to color B after 10 rows. (Color numbers will be specified in the pattern.)

Cast on 45 sts using the knit-on cast on method.

Row 1 (WS) Sl 1 purlwise, k to last st, p1.

Row 2 Sl 1 purlwise, p to center 3 sts, SK2P, p to end.

Row 3 Sl 1 purlwise, p to end.

Row 4 Sl 1 purlwise, k to center 3 sts, SK2P, k to last st, p1.

Rep rows 1–4 until you have 3 sts left.

Next Row SK2P.

Cut yarn, and slide tail through remaining loop.

4 CENTER SQUARES

Work these 4 squares using P121L as color A and P812 as color B.

Square 1 Follow square pattern. On the pillow, the decrease for square 1 will slant from bottom left to top right.

Square 2 With RS facing, pick up and knit 23 sts down left edge of square 1. Cast on 22 additional sts, then complete square.

Square 3 With RS facing, pick up and knit 23 sts across bottom edge of square 2. Cast on 22 additional sts, then complete square.

Square 4 With RS facing, pick up and knit 23 sts up right edge of square 3, and 22 more across bottom edge of square 1. Complete square.

8 SIDE EDGE SQUARES

Work these 8 squares using P121L as color A and P105L as color B.

Square 5 Cast on 22 sts, then pick up and knit 23 sts across top edge of square 1 with RS facing. Complete square.

Square 6 With RS facing, pick up and knit 23 sts across top edge of square 2, then cast on 22 additional sts. Attach this square to square 5 as you go, knitting the last st of every WS row together with the corresponding edge st on square 5.

Work squares 7–12 the same way.

4 CORNER SQUARES

Work these 4 squares using P812 as color A and P105L as color B.

Square 13 With RS facing, pick up and knit 23 sts across top edge of square 12, and 22 more along right edge of square 5. Complete square. Work squares 14–16 the same way.

2nd Side (shown in photo at left)

CENTER DIAMOND

Cast on 113 sts using P105L. Place marker on each corner.

Row 1 (RS) Sl 1, SKP, k24, *SK2P, k25; rep from * once more, SK2P, k24, k2tog, p1.

Row 2 Knit.

Row 3 Sl 1, SKP, *k22, SK2P, k23; rep from * once more, k22, k2tog, p1.

Row 4 Knit.

Row 5 Sl 1, SKP, *k20, SK2P, k21; rep from * once more, k20, k2tog, p1.

Row 6 Purl.

Row 7 Sl , SKP, *k18, SK2P, k19; rep from * once more, k18, k2tog, p1.

Row 8 Purl.

Continue in this manner, working 4 rows in garter st, then 4 rows in stockinette st, and decreasing on every RS row as established, until you have 9 sts left.

Next row K2tog 4 times, p1.

Cut yarn, and slide tail through remaining 5 sts. Sew the 2 open edges together using 2 needles and a crochet hook to form a diamond. On the pillow, this seam will be at the bottom corner of the diamond.

4 LARGE DIAMONDS

Use P812 for these diamonds.

Diamond 2 Cast on 28 sts, then pick up and knit 29 sts along top right edge of center diamond with RS facing.

Row 1 (WS) Sl 1 purlwise, p to end.

Row 2 Sl 1 purlwise, k to center 3 sts, SK2P, k to last st, p1.

Row 3 Sl 1 purlwise, k to last st, p1.

Row 4 Rep row 2.

Rep rows 1–4 until you have 5 sts left.

Next row K1, SK2P, k1.

Cut yarn, and slide tail through remaining 3 sts.

Diamond 3 Pick up and knit 29 sts along top left edge of center diamond with RS facing, then cast on 28 sts. Work diamond same as diamond 2.

Turn fabric upside down, and work diamonds 4 and 5 the same way.

4 SIDE EDGE TRIANGLES

Use P105L for these triangles.

Triangle 1 With RS facing, pick up and knit 29 sts across top left edge of diamond 2, and 28 more sts across top right edge of diamond 3.

Row 1 (WS) Purl.

Row 2 Sl 1, SKP, k to center 3 sts, SK2P, k to last 3 sts, k2tog, p1.

Row 3 Sl 1, k to last st, p1.

Row 4 Rep row 2.

Rep rows 1–4 until you have 5 sts left.

Next row K1, SK2P, k1.

Cut yarn, and slide tail through remaining 3 sts.

Work triangles 2–4 the same way.

4 CORNER TRIANGLES

Triangle 5 With RS facing, pick up and knit 29 sts across top right edge of diamond 2.

Row 1 (WS) Sl 1, work to last st, p1.

Row 2 Sl 1, k2tog, work to last 3 sts, SKP, p1.

Rep rows 1 and 2 until 5 sts rem.

Next row (RS) K2tog, k1, SKP. Work 1 row even.

Last row SK2P. Fasten off last st.

Triangle 6 With RS facing, pick up and knit 29 sts across top left edge of diamond 3. Complete as for triangle 5.

Work triangles 7 and 8 the same way.

FINISHING

Seam the two sides of the pillowcase together along 3 edges using two needles and a crochet hook. Insert pillow stuffing, then seam 4th edge. ◆

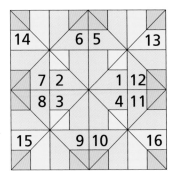

Pillow–1st Side

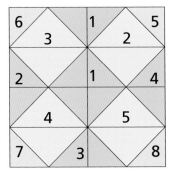

Pillow–2nd Side

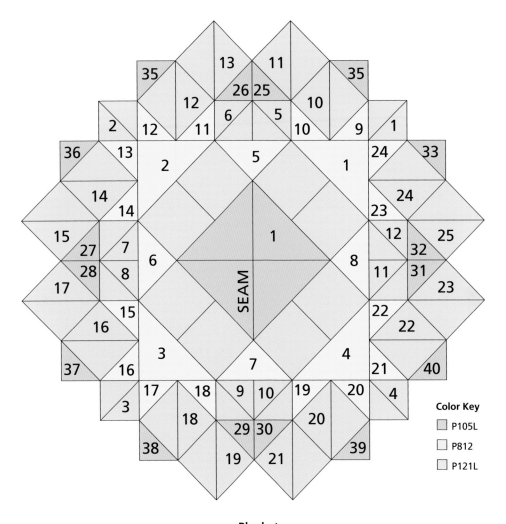

Color Key

- P105L
- P812
- P121L

Blanket

Blanket

KNITTED MEASUREMENTS

◆ 28x28"/71x71cm

MATERIALS

◆ 2 1.75oz/50g skeins of Koigu *Painter's Palette Premium Merino* (100% wool), 175yd/161m in each P105L, P121L, and P812
◆ Size US 3 (3.25mm) needles OR SIZE TO OBTAIN GAUGE
◆ Size D/3 (3mm) crochet hook, or size to correspond with needle
◆ Stitch markers

GAUGE

28 stitches and 36 rows = 4" (10cm) in stockinette stitch.
TAKE TIME TO CHECK GAUGE.

Note Cast on all sts using the knit-on cast on method. When picking up sts, always face the right side.

LARGE CENTER DIAMOND (PINK)

Cast on 240 sts using P105L.
Row 1 (RS) Sl 1, SKP, k57, *SK2P, k57; rep from * once more, k57, k2tog, p1.
Row 2 Knit.
Row 3 Sl 1, SKP, *k54, SK2P, k55; rep from * once more, k54, k2tog, p1.
Row 4 Knit.
Row 5 Sl 1, SKP, *k52, SK2P, k53; rep from * once more, k52, k2tog, p1.
Row 6 Purl.
Row 7 Sl 1, SKP, *k50, SK2P, k51; rep from * once more, k50, k2tog, p1.
Row 8 Purl.
Continue in this manner, working 4 rows in garter st, then 4 rows in stockinette st, and decreasing on every RS row as established, until you have 9 sts left.
Next row K2tog 4 times, k1.
Cut yarn, and slide tail through remaining 5 sts. Sew 2 open edges together using 2 needles and a crochet hook to form a diamond. On the blanket, this seam will be at the bottom corner of the diamond.
Place 4 stitch markers on the fabric, one to mark the center of each edge of diamond.

8 SMALL DIAMONDS (BLUE)

Use P121L for these diamonds.
Diamond 2 Cast on 29 sts. With RS facing, pick up and knit 30 more sts along top right edge of center diamond, beginning at right corner, and ending at marker.
Row 1 (WS) Sl 1 purlwise, k to last st, p1.
Row 2 Sl 1 purlwise, k to center 3 sts, SK2P, k to last st, p1.
Row 3 As row 1.
Row 4 As row 2.
Row 5 As row 1.
Row 6 As row 2.
Row 7 Sl 1 p wise, p to end.
Row 8 As row 2.

Repeat these 8 rows until you have 3 sts left.

Next row SK2P.

Cut yarn, and slide tail through remaining st.

Diamond 3 Pick up and knit 30 sts along top left edge of diamond 2, and 29 more sts along top right edge of center diamond, beginning at marker, and ending at top corner. Complete small diamond same as diamond 2.

Diamond 4 Pick up and knit 30 sts along top left edge of center diamond, beginning at marker and ending at left corner, then cast on 29 more sts. Complete small diamond same as diamond 2.

Diamond 5 Pick up and knit 30 sts along top left edge of center diamond, beginning at top corner and ending at marker, and 29 more sts along top right edge of diamond 4. Complete small diamond same as diamond 2.

Turn fabric upside down, and work diamonds 6–9 the same way.

4 CORNER TRIANGLES (YELLOW)

Use P812 for these triangles.

Triangle 1 Pick up and knit 59 sts along top right edges of diamonds 2 and 3.

Row 1 (WS) Knit.

Row 2 SKP, k to last 2 sts, k2tog.

Repeat these 2 rows until you have 3 sts left.

Next row K3tog.

Cut yarn, and slide tail through remaining st.

Work triangles 2–4 the same way.

4 SIDE EDGE TRIANGLES (YELLOW)

Use P812 for these triangles.

Triangle 5 Pick up and knit 30 sts along top left edge of diamond 2, and 29 more sts along top right edge of diamond 5.

Row 1 (WS) Knit.

Row 2 SKP, k to center 3 sts, SK2P, k to last 2 sts, k2tog.

Repeat these 2 rows until you have 3 sts left.

Next row K3tog.

Cut yarn, and slide tail through remaining st.

Work triangles 6–8 the same way.

16 MINI TRIANGLES (YELLOW)

Use P812 for these triangles.

Triangle 9 Pick up and knit 21 sts across right half of top edge of triangle 1.

Row 1 (WS) Knit.

Row 2 K to last 2 sts, k2tog.

Repeat these 2 rows until you have 1 st left.

Cut yarn, and slide tail through remaining st.

Triangle 10 Pick up and knit 21 sts across left half of top edge of triangle 1.

Row 1 (WS) Knit.

Row 2 SKP, k to end.

Repeat these 2 rows until you have 1 st left.

Cut yarn, and slide tail through remaining st.

Work triangles 11–24 the same way.

4 CORNER SQUARES (BLUE)

Use P121L for these squares

Square 1 Pick up and knit 21 sts across top edge of triangle 24, and 20 more sts up right edge of triangle 9.

Row 1 (WS) Sl 1 purlwise, k to last st, p1.

Row 2 Sl 1 purlwise, k to center 3 sts, SK2P, k to last st, p1.

Rep these 2 rows until you have 3 sts left.

Next row SK2P.

Cut yarn, and slide tail through remaining st.

Work squares 2–4 the same way.

8 SIDE EDGE SQUARES (BLUE)

Use P121L for these squares

Square 5 Pick up and knit 21 sts down left edge of triangle 10, and 20 more sts across right half of top edge of triangle 5. Complete square same as corner squares.

Square 6 Pick up and knit 21 sts across left half of top edge of triangle 5, and 20 more sts up right edge of triangle 11.

Row 1 (WS) Sl 1 purlwise, k to last st, k last st tog with corresponding edge st of square 5.

Row 2 Sl 1 purlwise, k to center 3 sts, SK2P, k to last st, p1.

Rep these 2 rows until you have 3 sts left.

Next row SK2P.

Cut yarn, and slide tail through remaining st.

Work squares 7–12 the same way.

8 MINI TRIANGLES (PINK)

Use P105L for these triangles.

Triangle 25 Pick up and knit 21 sts across top edge of square 5. Complete triangle same as triangle 10.

Triangle 26 Pick up and knit 21 sts across top edge of square 6.

Row 1 (WS) K to last st, k last st tog with corresponding edge st of triangle 25.

Row 2 K to last 2 sts, k2tog.

Repeat these 2 rows until you have 1 st left.

Cut yarn, and slide tail through remaining st.

Work triangles 27–32 the same way.

16 OUTER DIAMONDS (BLUE)

Use P121L for these diamonds.

Diamond 10 Pick up and knit 30 sts along left edge of triangle 9, and 29 more sts along right edge of triangle 10.

Row 1 (WS) Sl 1 purlwise, k to last st, p1.

Row 2 Sl 1 purlwise, k to center 3 sts, SK2P, k to last st, p1.

Repeat these 2 rows until you have 3 sts left.

Next row K3tog.

Cut yarn, and slide tail through remaining st.

Diamond 11 Pick up and knit 30 sts along top

left edge of diamond 10, and 29 more sts along right edge of triangle 25. Complete diamond same as diamond 10.

Diamond 12 Pick up and knit 30 sts along left edge of triangle 11, and 29 more sts along right edge of triangle 12. Complete diamond same as diamond 10.

Diamond 13 Pick up and knit 30 sts along left edge of triangle 26, and 29 more sts along top right edge of diamond 12. Complete diamond same as diamond 10.

Work diamonds 14–25 the same way.

8 OUTER MINI TRIANGLES (PINK)

Use P105L for these triangles.

Triangle 33 Pick up and knit 29 sts along top right edge of diamond 24.

Row 1 (WS) Knit.

Row 2 SKP, k to last 3 sts, k2tog, p1.

Repeat these 2 rows until you have 3 sts left.

Next row SK2P.

Cut yarn, and slide tail through remaining st.

Work triangles 34–40 the same way.

EDGING

Work 1 row in sc around entire blanket using P105L.

Next row *Sc in next 3 sc, ch 3, skip 1 sc; rep from * around.

Fasten off.

BLOCKING

Place blanket flat on a towel and pin to measurements. Spray with water and allow to dry. ◆

Dress

FINISHED MEASUREMENTS

◆ Bust 40"/102cm

◆ Length 24"/61cm (not including fringe)

MATERIALS

◆ 9 1.75oz/50g skeins of Koigu *Painter's Palette Premium Merino* (100% wool), 175yd/161m in P150

◆ 1 1.75oz/50g skein of Koigu *Premium Merino* (100% wool), 175yd/161m in 2132 (solid)

◆ Size US 3 (3.25mm) one pair and two dpn OR SIZE TO OBTAIN GAUGE

◆ Size D/3 (3mm) crochet hook, or size to correspond with needle

◆ 0.25"/0.5cm–wide elastic, long enough to fit around bust at underarms.

GAUGE

28 stitches and 36 rows = 4" (10cm) in stockinette stitch.
TAKE TIME TO CHECK GAUGE.

TECHNIQUES

See Stitch Workshop for:

◆ Joining seams with 2 needles and a crochet hook

Groovy Dress and Shawl
intermediate

Koigu's smooth, soft wool is ideal for all seasons. This bare-shouldered dress is perfect for summer evenings at the beach. A matching long, dressy shawl works perfectly with the dress. The Groovy Dress and Shawl are all about fun: fun color and fun style.

Note The dress is made of 36 separately knitted strips. For each strip, cast on 8 sts using P150, and work in stockinette stitch. When the strip measures anywhere between 36" and 43"/92cm and 110cm (try to vary the lengths), bind off all sts.

Join strips lengthwise with 2132 using two needles and a crochet hook (as shown in the Stitch Workshop). Vary the length of the seams between 28" and 24"/71cm and 61cm, allowing the remainder of the strip to hang down as fringe. Be sure to keep top edge of dress evenly lined up, and to face the RS of all strips the same way. Tie each strip into a knot about 1"/2.5cm from bottom end.

ELASTIC

Make another strip 40"/101.5cm in length using P150. Fold strip in half lengthwise around elastic and seam side edges together, at the same time seaming to top of dress.

NECK BAND

Create an i-cord 18"/45.5cm in length using P150. Sew ends of i-cord to front of dress at center, about 6"/15.5cm apart.

FINISHING

Weave in all ends at back of garment.

BLOCKING

Place dress flat on a towel and pin to measurements. Spray with water and allow to dry. ◆

Shawl

FINISHED MEASUREMENTS

◆ Approx 16" x 75"/40cm x 190cm (not including fringe)

MATERIALS

◆ 4 1.75oz/50g skeins of Koigu *Painter's Palette Premium Merino* (100% wool), 175yd/161m in P150

◆ Size US 6 (4mm) circular needle, 60"/150cm long (used as a straight needle) OR SIZE TO OBTAIN GAUGE

GAUGE

16 stitches and 16 rows = 4" (10cm) in drop stitch pattern.

TAKE TIME TO CHECK GAUGE.

SHAWL

Cast on 300 sts, leaving a 16"/40.5cm tail. Leave a 16"/40.5cm loop of yarn at the beginning and end of every row for fringe. Knit all sts in pattern through the back loop. Work in drop stitch patterns as follows:

Rows 1–4 Knit.

Row 5 K2, *yo 5 times, k1; rep from * to last 2 sts, yo 5 times, k2.

Row 6 K2, *drop 5 yos, k1; rep from * to last 2 sts, drop 5 yos, k2.

Rep rows 1–6 nine more times, then knit 4 more rows. Bind off all sts.

FRINGE

Tie together each group of tails at the edges of the garter st sections.

BLOCKING

Place shawl flat on a towel and pin to measurements, tugging widthwise to straighten loops. Spray with water and allow to dry. ◆

FINISHED MEASUREMENTS

◆ Bust 40 (44, 48)"/101.5 (111.5, 122)cm

◆ Length 14 (16.5, 19.5)"/35.5 (42, 49.5)cm

◆ Cardigan neck edge 18 (20, 20)"/46(51, 51) cm

MATERIALS

◆ 3 (4, 4) 1.75oz/50g skeins of Koigu *Painter's Palette Premium Merino* (100% wool), each 175yd/161m in P806

◆ 6 (6, 7) skeins in P823

◆ 5 (6, 6) skeins in P801

◆ Size US 3 (3.25mm) circular needle (used as a straight needle), 40"/100cm long OR SIZE TO OBTAIN GAUGE

◆ Size US 0 (2mm) circular needle (used as a straight needle), 24"/60cm long

◆ 7 (8, 9) buttons

◆ Stitch holders

GAUGE

28 stitches and 36 rows = 4" (10cm) in stockinette stitch using larger needle.

TAKE TIME TO CHECK GAUGE.

Jazz Cardigan (Adult)
experienced

Each Koigu handpaint is attractive alone, and combining them within a knitted piece is exciting. Maie Landra uses color in her knitting designs as she does in her watercolor paintings. Koigu Jazz incorporates three different variegated yarns.

ZIGZAG PATTERN

(multiple of 12 sts plus 3)

Row 1 (RS) K1, SKP, *k9, sl 2, k1, p2sso; rep from * to last 12 sts, end k9, k2tog, k1.

Row 2 (WS) K1, *p1, k4, (k1, yo, k1) in next st, k4; rep from * to last 2 sts, end p1, k1.

Work rows 1 and 2 twice for pattern.

BODY

With larger needle and P823 cast on 315 (339, 363) sts. Work 4 rows in garter st.

Work in zigzag pattern for 2"/5cm using P823. Change to P801 and work 2"/5cm more in pat. Change to P806, and work 0.5"/1cm more in pat. Continue in zigzag pattern, changing colors in this manner until piece measures 14 (14, 18)"/35.5 (35.5, 45.5)cm from beg.

Divide for armhole

Place first and last 79 (85, 91) sts on holders for front panels. Cut yarn. Center 157 (169, 181) sts remain on the needle for back panel.

BACK

Attach yarn to center back panel sts and work in pat for 8 (9, 9)"/20 (23, 23)cm, changing colors as before.

Divide for neck

Work 52 (56, 60) sts, place next 53 (57, 61) sts on a stitch holder for neck, attach 2nd ball of yarn and work to end. Working both sides at once, work even for 1"/2.5cm. Bind off sts each side for shoulders.

RIGHT FRONT

With RS facing, join yarn and work across 79 (85, 91) sts from right front panel holder and work in patterns, changing colors to correspond to back, for 7.5 (8.5, 8.5)"/19 (21.5, 21.5)cm, end with a WS row.

Next row (RS) Work across 27 (29, 31) sts and place on holder for neck, work to end. Work even on these 52 (56, 60) sts until same length as back to shoulder. Bind off.

LEFT FRONT

Work to correspond to right front, reversing shaping.

SLEEVES

With larger needle and P823 cast on 63 sts. Work 4 rows in garter st. Work in zigzag pattern, changing colors as before, and at the same time increase 1 st at each end of needle every 5th row until you have 123 (135, 135) sts. Continue evenly in pattern until piece measures 21 (21, 22)"/53 (53, 56)cm from beg. Bind off.

COLLAR

With RS facing, smaller needle and P823, knit across 27 (29, 31) sts from right front holder, pick up and knit 14 (16, 18) sts along neck edge, knit across 53 (57, 61) sts from back neck holder, pick up and knit 14 (16, 18) sts along neck edge, knit across 27 (29, 31) sts from left front holder—135 (147, 159) sts.

Work in zigzag pattern for 1.5 (1.5, 2)"/4 (4, 5)cm, then work 4 rows in garter st. Bind off.

LEFT FRONT BAND

With smaller needle and P823, cast on 15 sts, and work in zigzag pattern until piece measures 23 (24, 28.5)"/58.5 (61, 72.5)cm. Bind off. Sew band to left front edge.

RIGHT FRONT BAND

Work as left band for 1.5"/4cm, then make a buttonhole as follows:

Next row (RS) K1, SKP, k4, k1 wrapping yarn twice, k4, k2tog, k1.

Next row K1, p1, k4, (k1, yo, k1) in next st dropping extra loop, k4, p1, k1.

Repeat buttonhole every 3"/7.5cm until piece measures 23 (24, 28.5)"/58.5 (61, 72.5)cm—7 (8, 9) buttonholes. Bind off. Sew band to right front edge.

With center of bound-off sts of sleeves at shoulder seams, sew tops of sleeves to front and back. Sew sleeve seams. Sew buttons to left front band, corresponding to buttonholes.

BLOCKING

Place cardigan flat on towel and pin to measurements. Spray with warm water and allow to dry. ◆

FINISHED MEASUREMENTS

◆ Children's sizes 4 (6, 8)

◆ Chest 26 (29, 32)"/66 (73.5, 81)cm

◆ Length 14 (16.5, 19.5)"/35.5 (42, 49.5)cm

MATERIALS

◆ 2 (3, 3) 1.75oz/50g skeins of Koigu *Painter's Palette Premium Merino* (100% wool), each 175yd/161m in P122

◆ 1 (2, 2) skeins each in P131 & P107

◆ Size US 3 (3.25mm) circular needle (used as straight needles) 24–32"/60–80cm long, OR SIZE TO OBTAIN GAUGE

◆ Size US 0 (2mm) circular needle, 24–32"/60–80cm long

◆ 5 (5, 6) 0.5"/1cm buttons

◆ Stitch holders

GAUGE

28 stitches and 36 rows = 4" (10cm) in stockinette stitch using larger needles.
TAKE TIME TO CHECK GAUGE.

Jazz Cardigan (Kids)
experienced

ZIGZAG PATTERN

(multiple of 12 sts plus 3)

Row 1 (RS) K1, SKP, *k9, sl 2, k1, p2sso, rep from * to last 12 sts, end k9, k2tog, k1.

Row 2 (WS) K1, *p1, k4, (k1, yo, k1) in next st, k4, rep from * to last 2 sts, end p1, k1.

Work rows 1 and 2 twice for pattern.

BODY

With larger needle and P122, cast on 183 (207, 231) sts. Work 4 rows in garter st.

Work in zigzag pattern with P122 for 2"/5cm. Change to P107 and work in pat for 2"/5cm more. Change to P131 work in pat for 2"/5cm more. Continue in zigzag pattern, changing colors in this manner until piece measures 8 (10, 12)"/20.5 (25.5, 30.5)cm.

Divide for armhole

Place first and last 46 (52, 58) sts on stitch holders for front panels. Cut yarn.

Center 91 (103, 115) sts remain on the needle for back panel.

BACK

Attach yarn to center back panel and work for 5 (5.5, 6)"/12.5 (14, 15)cm, changing colors as before.

Divide for neck

Work 30 (34, 38) sts, place next 31 (35, 39) sts on a stitch holder for neck, attach 2nd ball of yarn and work to end. Working both sides at once, work even for 1"/2.5cm. Bind off sts each side for shoulders.

RIGHT FRONT

With RS facing, join yarn and work across 46 (52, 58) sts from right front panel holder and work in patterns, changing colors to correspond to back, for 4.5 (5, 5.5)"/11.5 (12.5, 14)cm, end with a WS row.

Next row (RS) Work across 16 (18, 20) sts and place on holder for neck, work to end. Work even on these 30 (34, 38) sts until same length as back to shoulder. Bind off.

LEFT FRONT

Work to correspond to right front, reversing shaping.

SLEEVES

With larger needle and P122, cast on 51 sts. Work 4 rows in garter st. Work in zigzag pattern, changing colors as before, and at the same time increase 1 st at each end of needle every 4th row until you have 87 (99, 111) sts. Continue evenly in pattern until piece measures 13 (14, 15)"/33 (35.5, 38)cm from beg. Bind off.

COLLAR

With RS facing, smaller needle and P122, knit across 16 (18, 20) sts from right front holder, pick up and knit 18 (20, 22) sts along neck edge, knit across 31 (35, 39) sts from back neck holder, pick up and knit 18 (20, 22) sts along neck edge, knit across 16 (18, 20) sts from left front holder—99 (111, 123) sts.

Work in zigzag pattern for 1.5 (1.5, 2)"/4 (4, 5)cm, then work 4 rows in garter st. Bind off.

LEFT FRONT BAND

With smaller needle and P122, cast on 15 sts, and work in zigzag pattern until piece fits along left front edge. Bind off. Sew band to left front edge.

RIGHT FRONT BAND

Work as left band for 1.5"/4cm, then make a buttonhole as follows:

Next RS row K1, SKP, k4, k1 wrapping yarn twice, k4, k2tog, k1.

Next row K1, p1, k4, (k1, yo, k1) in next st dropping extra loop, k4, p1, k1.

Repeat buttonhole every 3"/7.5cm until there are 5 (5, 6) buttonholes. When band fits along right front edge, bind off. Sew band to right front edge.

With the center of bound-off sts of sleeves at shoulder seams, sew tops of sleeves to front and back. Sew sleeve seams. Sew buttons to left front band, corresponding to buttonholes.

BLOCKING

Place cardigan flat on towel and pin to measurements. Spray with water and allow to dry. ◆

FINISHED MEASUREMENTS

◆ 11" x 92"/28cm x 233.5cm

MATERIALS

◆ 3 1.75oz/50g skeins of Koigu *Painter's Palette Premium Merino* (100% wool), each 175yd/161m in P204

◆ Size US 3 (3.25mm) needles OR SIZE TO OBTAIN GAUGE

GAUGE

16 stitches and 12 rows = 4" (10cm) in drop stitch pattern.

TAKE TIME TO CHECK GAUGE.

Knit Yarn-Over Scarf
easy

This scarf is a very easy, quick knit. Let one variegated yarn create a beautiful pattern for you. Every scarf will be different!

SCARF

Cast on 40 stitches.

Work 4 rows in garter st.

Work in drop st pat as foll:

Row 1 K2, *yo, k1; rep from * to last 2 sts, k2.

Row 2 K2, *drop yo, k1; rep from * to last 2 sts, k2.

Rep rows 1 and 2 for drop st pat until scarf measures 91.5"/232cm in length (pull scarf lengthwise to straighten loops).

Work 4 more rows in garter st. Bind off loosely.

BLOCKING

Place scarf flat on a towel and pin to measurements, straightening loops. Spray with water and allow to dry. ◆

Skirt

FINISHED MEASUREMENTS

◆ Width at lower edge 60"/152cm

◆ Waist 25"/63.5 cm. This measurement can be
   adjusted to be smaller or larger with the
   waistband elastic

◆ Length 37"/94cm

MATERIALS

◆ 3 1.75oz/50g balls (each approx 176yd/160m)
   of Koigu Wool Designs KPM (wool) in
   #2169 navy (A)

◆ 2 balls each in #1153 lilac (B), #1400 royal (C) and
   #3000 dk plum (D)

◆ 2 1.75oz/50g balls (each approx 176yd/160m) of
   Koigu Wool Designs KPPPM (wool) each in #P829B
   purple (E), #P129B pink (F), #P807B rose (G),
   #P831D peach (H) and #P805 dk purple (I)

◆ One set (4) dpn size 3 (3.25mm) OR SIZE TO
   OBTAIN GAUGE

◆ Two size 3 (3.25mm) circular needles 40"/100cm
   long

◆ Approx 1yd/1m of ½"/1.5cm-wide waistband elastic

◆ Tapestry needle

GAUGE

28 sts and 36 rows = 4" (10cm) over St st using size 3
(3.25mm) needles.

TAKE TIME TO CHECK GAUGE.

Spirit **Skirt with Sweater**
experienced

The Spirit Skirt is dedicated to Maie's late husband, Harry. The hexagon in the skirt, with its subtle colors, symbolizes his life: many complexities unite in a seamless whole. The sweater is made from vertical strips joined with contrasting yarn. It features unusual ruffles at the neck, sleeves and edge.

TECHNIQUES
See Stitch Workshop for:
◆ Joining seams with 2 needles and a crochet hook

SAMPLE HEXAGON
Note Make a sample hexagon using the instructions below before starting skirt hexagons. The skirt begins at the top, with the smallest size hexagon, and works down to the lower edge. The hexagons become larger as you work downward.

Segment 1
Cast on 25 sts.
Row 1 (WS) K to last st, p1.
Row 2 Sl 1, k10, SK2P, k10, p1.
Row 3 Sl 1, k9, SK2P, k9, p1.
Row 4 Sl 1, k8, SK2P, k8, p1.
Row 5 Sl 1, k7, SK2P, k7, p1.
Row 6 Sl 1, k6, SK2P, k6, p1.
Row 7 Sl 1, k5, SK2P, k5, p1.
Row 8 Sl 1, k4, SK2P, k4, p1.
Row 9 Sl 1, k3, SK2P, k3, p1.
Row 10 Sl 1, k2, SK2P, k2, p1.
Row 11 Sl 1, k1, SK2P, k1, p1.
Row 12 Sl 1, SK2P, p1.
Row 13 SK2P.
Row 14 K1, cut yarn and pull through loop.

Segment 2
Pick up 13 sts along side of segment 1, cast on 12 sts—25 sts. Work as for segment 1.
Segment 3
Pick up 13 sts along side of segment 2. Cast on 12 sts—25 sts. Work as for segment 1.
Segment 4
Pick up 13 sts along side of segment 3. Cast on 12 sts—25 sts. Work as for segment 1.
Segment 5
Pick up 13 sts along side of segment 4. Cast on 12 sts—25 sts. Work as for segment 1.
Segment 6
Pick up 13 sts along side of segment 5 and 12 sts from segment 1—25 sts. Work as for segment 1.

JOINING HEXAGONS
With RS facing and A, pick up sts along one side edge of hexagon and leave sts on dpn. Pick up sts along side edge of another hexagon. Use 2 needles and a crochet hook to join them tog.
Notes The skirt consists of six horizontal strips, and each strip has 9 hexagons. Follow the color distribution diagram for color placement.
Make the 9 hexagons separately, then join them tog with 2 needles and a crochet hook. After all horizontal strips have been joined, join them into six vertical rows as described under "Joining strips".

TOP OF SKIRT
Horizontal Strip 1
(make 9 hexagons)
Cast on 29 sts for segment 1.
Row 1 K to last st, p1.
Row 2 Sl 1, k12, SK2P, k12, p1. Complete as for segment 1. For segment 2, pick up 15 sts along side of segment 1, cast on 14 sts—29 sts. Complete as for sample hexagon. Work 8 more hexagons, then join all nine to form strip as described above.
Horizontal Strip 2
(make 9 hexagons)
Cast on 33 sts for segment 1.
Row 1 K to last st, p1.
Row 2 Sl 1, k14, SK2P, k14, p1. Complete as for segment 1. For segment 2, pick up 17 sts along side of segment 1, cast on 16 sts—33 sts. Complete as for sample hexagon. Work 8 more hexagons, then join all nine to form strip as described above.
Horizontal Strip 3
(make 9 hexagons)

Hexagon Skirt
Color Placement Diagrams

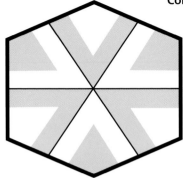

Hexagon strips 1 and 3

Each hexagon has 2 solid colors and
one variegated color. Use colors at random.
The shaded areas (half segment) are variegated;
the blank areas (other half of segment) are solid.

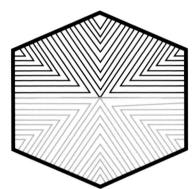

Hexagon strips 2, 4 and 5

Each hexagon has 2 solid colors and one
variegated color. Use colors at random.
The black lines represent 2 rows of one solid
color, the grey lines represent 2 rows of a
2nd solid color and the blank spaces in between
represent 2 rows of the variegated color.

Hexagon strip 6

Each hexagon has 2 solid colors and
one variegated color. Use colors at random.
The darker areas represent 4 rows of
one solid color; the lighter areas represent
4 rows of the 2nd solid color; the blank
area represents 4 rows of the variegated.

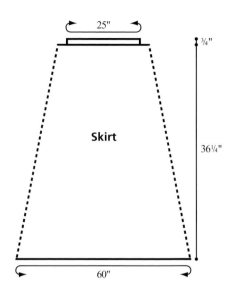

Skirt

25"

¾"

36¼"

60"

Placement Diagram

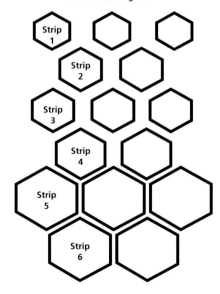

Cast on 37 sts for segment 1.

Row 1 K to last st, p1.

Row 2 Sl 1, k16, SK2P, k16, p1. Complete as for sample hexagon. For segment 2, pick up 19 sts along side of segment 1, cast on 18 sts—37 sts. Complete as for sample hexagon. Work 8 more hexagons, then join all nine to form strip as described above.

Horizontal Strip 4

(make 9 hexagons)

Cast on 41 sts for segment 1.

Row 1 K to last st, p1.

Row 2 Sl 1, k18, SK2P, k18, p1. Complete as for segment 1. For segment 2, pick up 21 sts along side of segment 1, cast on 20 sts—41 sts. Complete as for sample hexagon. Work 8 more hexagons, then join all nine to form strip as described above.

Horizontal Strip 5

(make 9 hexagons)

Cast on 45 sts for segment 1.

Row 1 K to last st, p1.

Row 2 Sl 1, k20, SK2P, k20, p1. Complete as for sample hexagon. For segment 2, pick up 23 sts along side of segment 1, cast on 22 sts—45 sts. Complete as for sample hexagon. Work 8 more hexagons, then join all nine to form strip as described above.

Horizontal Strip 6

Work same as horizontal strip 5.

Lower edge border

With RS facing, circular needle and A, pick up and k sts evenly along one long edge of horizontal strip 6. Join and work in rev St st for 6 rnds. Bind off loosely. Edge will roll to WS.

Joining strips

With RS facing, circular needle and A, pick up and k sts evenly along top of strip 6. Count the number of sts. Join and p 1 rnd. Keep sts on needle. With RS facing, circular needle and A, pick up and k the same number of sts along edge of strip 5, join and p 1 rnd. With WS of both strips facing each other (that is, purl side of border is showing), join two strips tog using 2 needles and a crochet hook.

With RS facing, circular needle and A, pick up and k sts evenly along edge of strip 4. Count the number of sts. Join and p 2 rnds. Keep sts on needle. With RS facing, circular needle and A, pick up and k sts evenly along top of strip 5, join and p 2 rnds, decreasing sts evenly over these two rnds so that final number matches sts on strip 4. Join with 2 needles and a crochet hook as before.

With RS facing, circular needle and A, pick up and k sts evenly along edge of strip 3. Count the number of sts. Join and p 3 rnds. Keep sts on needle. With RS facing, circular needle and A, pick up and k sts evenly along top of strip 4, join and p 3 rnds, decreasing sts evenly over these three rnds so that final number matches sts on strip 3. Join with 2 needles and a crochet hook. Join strips 2 and 3 same as strips 3 and 4. With RS facing, circular needle and A, pick up and k sts evenly along edge of strip 1. Count the number of sts. Join and p 4 rnds. Keep sts on needle. With RS facing, circular needle and A, pick up and k sts evenly along top of strip 2, join and p 4 rnds, decreasing sts evenly over these four rnds so that final number matches sts on strip 1. Join with 2 needles and a crochet hook as before.

Waistband

With RS facing, circular needle and A, pick up and k sts evenly along top of strip 1. Join and work in St st for 12 rows. Fold facing in half to WS and sew.

Open sts in place for casing, leaving an opening for elastic. Thread elastic through facing, adjust to desired waist width and sew opening closed.

FINISHING

Place skirt flat on a towel and pin to measurements. Spray with water and allow to dry. ◆

Sweater

FINISHED MEASUREMENTS

- Bust 36"/92cm
- Length 21"/53cm

MATERIALS

- 7 1.75oz/50g skeins of Koigu *Premium Merino* (100% wool), 175yd/161m in 2169
- 1 skein in 3000
- Size US 3 (3.25mm) circular needle (used as straight needles) OR SIZE TO OBTAIN GAUGE
- Set of double-pointed needles in same size
- Size D/3 (3mm) crochet hook, or size to correspond with needle
- Stitch holders

GAUGE

28 stitches and 36 rows = 4" (10cm) in stockinette stitch.

TAKE TIME TO CHECK GAUGE.

BODY

Work 32 separate strips using 2169 as follows:

Cast on 4 sts.

Row 1 (RS) K1, M1, k to last st, M1, k1.

Row 2 Purl.

Rep these 2 rows until you have 12 sts.

Next 2 rows:

Row 1 K1, SKP, k to last 3 sts, k2tog, k1.

Row 2 Purl.

Rep these 2 rows once more (8 sts).

Next 2 rows:

Row 1 Sl 1 purlwise, k to last st, p1.

Row 2 Sl 1 purlwise, p to end.

Rep these 2 rows until strip measures 14"/35.5cm in length. Bind off all sts.

Join the strips lengthwise into a tube to make the body with 3000 using 2 needles and a crochet hook. Be sure to keep top of strips (cast-on edges) evenly lined up, and to face the RS of all strips the same way.

FRONT

With RS facing and 2169, pick up and knit 120 sts evenly across the tops (bound-off edges) of 15 strips.

Row 1 (WS) Knit.

Row 2 Purl.

Row 3 Knit.

Row 4 Knit.

Row 5 Purl.

Continue in stockinette stitch for 5"/12.5cm.

Divide for neck Place center 30 sts on a stitch holder. Work each shoulder separately, decreasing 1 st at neck edge every RS row 5 times—40 sts each shoulder. Continue evenly for a total of 7"/18cm in stockinette st, then place all sts on a stitch holder.

BACK

With RS facing and 2169, pick up and knit 120 sts across the tops of center 15 strips on opposite side. Leave 1 strip unworked at each end for armhole.

Row 1 (WS) Knit.

Row 2 Purl.

Row 3 Knit.

Row 4 Knit.

Row 5 Purl.

Continue in stockinette stitch for 6"/15cm.

Divide for neck Place center 34 sts on a stitch holder. Work each shoulder separately, decreasing 1 st at neck edge every RS row 3 times—40 sts each shoulder. Continue evenly for a total of 7"/18cm in stockinette st.

Join front and back shoulders using 3-needle bind off with right sides facing together.

SLEEVES

Make 2 strips for each sleeve as follows:

Cast on 4 sts using 2169.

Row 1 (RS) K1, M1, k to last st, M1, k1.

Row 2 Purl.

Rep rows 1 and 2 until you have 26 sts.

Next 6 rows

Rows 1 and 3 Knit.

Rows 2, 4, and 6 Purl.

Row 5 K1, m1, k to end.

Rep rows 1–6 until you have 42 sts. On 2nd strip, work increases at left edge instead of right edge.

Continue evenly until strip measures 20"/51cm, then bind off all sts.

Make one 20"/51cm strip for each sleeve, worked same as body strips (8 sts across).

Join the 3 strips together lengthwise with 3000 using 2 needles and a crochet hook, being sure to place the narrow strip in the center, and the increased edges on the outside.

Sew together increased edges of sleeves using 2169 and working in mattress stitch.

Sew sleeves to body.

NECK RUFFLE

With circular needle and 2169, knit across 30 sts from front neck holder, pick up and knit 20 sts up right neck edge, knit across 34 sts from back neck holder, pick up and knit 20 sts down left neck edge (104 sts). Join round, and work 10 rnds in stockinette st.

Ruffle Petals

Row 1 K8, turn work.

Row 2 P8, turn work.

Row 3 K1, SKP, k to last 3 sts, k2tog, k1.

Row 4 Purl.

Rep rows 3 and 4 once more.

Next row K2tog twice.

Cut yarn, and slide tail through remaining 2 loops.

Work 12 more petals around neck the same way.

BLOCKING

Place sweater flat on a towel and pin to measurements. Spray with water and allow to dry. ◆

FINISHED MEASUREMENTS

◆ 6" x 56"/15cm x 142cm

MATERIALS

◆ 1 1.75oz/50g skein of Koigu *Painter's Palette Premium Merino* (100% wool), 175yd/161m in each P105L, P105D, P142, and P111

◆ Size US 3 (3.25mm) needles OR SIZE TO OBTAIN GAUGE

GAUGE

28 sts and 36 rows to 4" (10cm) over stockinette st using size 3 (3.25mm) needles.
TAKE TIME TO CHECK GAUGE.

TECHNIQUES

See Stitch Workshop for:

◆ Casting on

◆ Practice square

◆ Picking up stitches

◆ Changing direction of decreases

Basic Squares Scarf
intermediate

The Basic Squares Scarf is a great small project to familiarize you with the modular knitting technique. Mitered squares, patchwork, or domino knitting—whatever you choose to call it, it offers limitless possibilities! Once you've mastered the basics, you'll find it highly addictive.

BASIC SQUARE

Note Knit all sts through the back loop.

Cast on 25 sts using the knit-on cast on method.

Row 1 (WS) K24, p1.

Row 2 Sl 1 knitwise (edge), k10, SK2P, k10, p1.

Row 3 Sl 1, k10, p1, k10, p1.

Row 4 Sl 1, k9, SK2P, k9, p1.

Rep rows 3 and 4, decreasing 2 sts in the center every RS row, until 3 sts remain, ending with a RS row.

Next Row (WS) Sl 1, p2tog, psso. Leave one open loop.

1ST ROW OF SQUARES

Using P105L, cast on 25 sts and work a basic square (square 1). On the scarf, the decreases in square 1 slant from bottom left to top right. Leave one open loop and remove needle. With RS facing, pick up 12 sts up right edge of square 1. Knit the open loop. Then cast on 12 more sts—25 sts. Work basic square (square 2). The decreases in square 2 slant from top left to bottom right. Leave one open loop and remove needle. Break off yarn. With RS facing, knit-cast on 12 sts, then knit the open loop. Pick up and knit 12 sts up the right

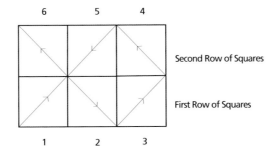

Second Row of Squares

First Row of Squares

edge of square 2—25 sts. Work basic square (square 3). The decreases in square 3 slant in the same direction as square 1. Cut yarn, and slide tail through remaining loop.

2ND ROW OF SQUARES

Using P142, knit-cast on 12 sts. Pick up and knit 13 sts from top of square 3, ending at inner edge of scarf. Work another basic square (square 4). The decreases in square 4 slant from bottom right to top left. Leave one open loop and remove needle. Break off yarn.

With RS facing, knit-cast on 12 sts, and knit the open loop. Pick up and knit 12 sts down left edge of square 4. Work another basic square (square 5). The decreases in square 5 slant from top right to bottom left. Attach this square to square 2 by knitting the last st of every RS row

together with a top edge st from square 2. Leave one open loop and remove needle. With RS facing, pick up 12 sts down left edge of square 5. Pick up open loop. Pick up and knit 12 sts from top edge of square 1—25 sts. Work another basic square (square 6). The decreases in square 6 slant from bottom right to top left. Cut yarn, and slide tail through remaining loop.

REMAINDER OF SCARF

Continue in established pattern. For every row of squares, change colors, and reverse direction of decreases.

EDGING

Pick up and knit 13 sts using P105D at each of the 3 squares at both ends of the scarf. Work in garter st, decreasing 1 st at each end of needle on every other row, until you have 3 sts. Work SK2P, cut yarn, and slide tail through remaining loop.

BLOCKING

Place scarf flat on a towel and pin to measurements. Spray with water and allow to dry. ◆

FINISHED MEASUREMENTS

◆ Bust 48 (64)"/122 (162)cm

◆ Length 19 (20)"/48 (50)cm

MATERIALS

◆ 8 (9) 1.75oz/50g skeins of Koigu *Painter's Palette Premium Merino* (100% wool), 175yd/161m in P105

◆ 5 (5) skeins in color P608

◆ 3 (4) skeins in color P102

◆ 1 1.75oz/50g skein of Koigu *Premium Merino* (100% wool), 175yd/161m in 2239 (solid)

◆ Size US 3 (3.25mm) needles OR SIZE TO OBTAIN GAUGE

◆ Size D.3 (3mm) crochet hook, or size to correspond with needle

◆ 5 latch-style clasps

GAUGE

28 stitches and 36 rows = 4" (10cm) in stockinette stitch.

TAKE TIME TO CHECK GAUGE.

TECHNIQUES

See Stitch Workshop for:

◆ Practice square

◆ Triangles

◆ Changing direction of decreases

◆ Joining seams with 2 needles and a crochet hook

Toreador Jacket
experienced

The Toreador Jacket (large size pictured) is for the adventurous knitter. It has wide sleeves, a mandarin collar and i-cord trim. Its symmetrical design uses three different-size squares in three different colorways. Be sure to make a practice swatch before beginning the pattern.

Notes Work left front first. Continue with left back, joining the squares along the top of the shoulder and arm. Make sure the decreases go in the opposite direction (see Stitch Workshop). After completing left back panel, join right back panel at center back, again changing the direction of decreases. Continue with right front, joining top of shoulder and arm as for left side, and again changing the direction of decreases.

Work the squares on the charts in the following colors:

Purple squares—use P102

Pink squares—use P608

Rose squares—use P105

The diagonal lines show the direction of the decreases. Whenever you pick up sts with WS facing to begin a square, start the square pattern on row 2.

To fasten off a square, cut yarn, and slide tail through remaining loop.

SMALL SQUARE PATTERN

(1" x 1"/2.5cm x 2.5cm)

Cast on 13 sts using the knit-on cast on method.

Row 1 (WS) Sl 1 purlwise, k to last st, p1.

Row 2 Sl 1 purlwise, k to center 3 sts, SK2P, k to last st, p1.

Rep rows 1 and 2 until you have 3 sts left.

Next row SK2P.

MEDIUM SQUARE PATTERN

(2" x 2"/5cm x 5cm)

Cast on 25 sts using the knit-on cast on method.

Row 1 (WS) Sl 1 purlwise, k to last st, p1.

Row 2 Sl 1 purlwise, k to center 3 sts, SK2P, k to last st, p1.

Rep these 2 rows 5 more times.

Next 2 rows:

Row 1 Sl 1 purlwise, k to last st, p1.

Row 2 Sl 1 purlwise, k to center 3 sts, SK2P, k to last st, p1.

Rep these 2 rows until you have 3 sts left.

Next row SK2P.

LARGE SQUARE PATTERN

(4" x 4"/10cm x 10cm)

Cast on 49 sts using the knit-on cast on method.

Row 1 (WS) Sl 1 purlwise, k to last st, p1.

Row 2 Sl 1 purlwise, k to center 3 sts, SK2P, k to last st, p1.

Rep these 2 rows 11 more times.

Next 2 rows:

Row 1 Sl 1 purlwise, p to end.

Row 2 Sl 1 purlwise, k to center 3 sts, SK2P, k to last st, p1.

Rep these 2 rows until you have 3 sts left.

Next row SK2P.

TRIANGLE PATTERN

Row 1 K to last 3 sts, k2tog, p1.

Row 2 K to last st, k last st together with edge st of corresponding square.

Rep these 2 rows until you have 2 sts left.

Next row K2tog.

SMALL JACKET

LEFT FRONT/RIGHT BACK

(make both pieces the same)

Square 1 Follow small square pattern. Fasten off.

Square 2 Work as square 1, but leave last loop on needle to pick up for next square.

Square 3 With RS facing, pick up and knit 6 up right edge of square 2. Cast on 6 more sts, and complete small square. Leave last loop on the needle.

Work squares 4 and 5 the same way.

Square 6 With RS facing, pick up 6 sts up right edge of square 5, and 6 more across bottom edge of square 1. Complete small square. Fasten off.

Square 7 With WS facing, pick up and knit 7 sts across bottom edge of square 2, then cast on 6 more sts. Complete small square. Leave last loop on the needle.

Square 8 With WS facing, pick up and knit 6 sts across bottom edge of square 7, then cast on 6 more sts. Complete small square. Leave last loop on the needle.

Work squares 9–13 the same way. Fasten off.

Square 14 With RS facing, pick up and knit 13 sts up right edges of squares 6 and 1, then cast on 12 more sts. Complete medium square. Fasten off.

Square 15 With RS facing, pick up and knit 13 sts up right edges of squares 8 and 7, and 12 more across bottom edges of squares 3 and 4. Complete medium square. Leave last loop on the needle.

Square 16 With RS facing, pick up and knit 12 sts up right edge of square 15, and 12 more across bottom edges of squares 5 and 6. Complete medium square. Leave last loop on the needle.

Work square 17 the same way. Fasten off.

Square 18 With WS facing, pick up and knit 13 sts across bottom edge of square 15, and 12 more down right edge of squares 9 and 10. Complete medium square. Leave last loop on the needle.

Square 19 With WS facing, pick up and knit 12 sts across bottom edge of square 18, and 12 more down right edge of squares 11 and 12. Complete medium square. Fasten off.

Square 20 With RS facing, pick up and knit 25 sts up right edges of squares 17 and 14. Cast on 24 more sts, then follow large square pattern. Fasten off.

Square 21 With RS facing, pick up and knit 25 sts up right edges of squares 19 and 18, and 24 more across bottom edges of squares 16 and 17.

Complete large square. Leave last loop on the needle.

Square 22 With RS facing, pick up and knit 24 sts up right edge of square 21, and 24 more across bottom edges of square 20. Complete large square. Fasten off.

Square 23 Cast on 6 sts, then with WS facing, pick up and knit 7 sts down first 1"/2.5cm of right edge of square 20. Complete small square. Leave last loop on the needle.

Square 24 With WS facing, pick up and knit 6 sts across bottom edge of square 23, and 6 more down next 1"/2.5cm of right edge of square 20. Complete small square. Leave last loop on the needle.

Work squares 25–30 the same way. Fasten off.

Square 31 With RS facing, pick up and knit 7 sts up right edge of square 13, and 6 more across first 1"/2.5cm of bottom edge of square 19. Complete small square. Leave last loop on the needle.

Square 32 With RS facing, pick up and knit 6 sts up right edge of square 31, and 6 more across 2nd 1"/2.5cm of bottom edge of square 19. Complete small square. Leave last loop on the needle.

Work squares 33–41 the same way. Fasten off.

Square 42 Cast on 12 sts, then with RS facing, pick up and knit 13 sts across bottom edges of squares 13 and 31. Complete medium square. Leave last loop on the needle.

Square 43 With RS facing, pick up and knit 12 sts up right edge of square 42, then 12 more across bottom edges of square 32 and 33. Complete medium square. Leave last loop on the needle.

Work squares 44–47 the same way. Fasten off.

Square 48 Cast on 25 sts, then with RS facing, pick up and knit 24 sts across bottom edges of squares 42 and 43. Complete large square. Leave last loop on the needle.

Square 49 With RS facing, pick up and knit 24 sts up right edge of square 48, then 24 more across bottom edges of square 44 and 45. Complete large square. Leave last loop on the needle.

Work square 50 the same way. Fasten off.

Square 51 Cast on 7 sts, then with RS facing, pick up and knit 6 sts across first 1"/2.5cm of bottom edge of square 48. Complete small square. Leave last loop on needle.

Square 52 With RS facing, pick up and knit 6 sts up right edge of square 51, and 6 more across 2nd 1"/2.5cm of bottom edge of square 48. Complete small square. Leave last loop on needle.

Work squares 53–62 the same way. Fasten off.

Work squares 63–68 same as 42–47.

Square 69 With RS facing, pick up and knit 7 sts up right edge of square 23, then cast on 6 more sts. Complete small square. Leave last loop on needle.

Work Squares 70–81 same as 3–5. Fasten off.

Square 82 With WS facing, pick up and knit 13 sts across bottom edges of squares 69 and 70, and 12 more down the right edges of squares 24 and 25. Complete medium square. Leave last loop on needle.

Square 83 With WS facing, pick up and knit 12 sts across bottom edge of square 82, and 12 more down right edges of squares 26 and 27. Complete medium square. Leave last loop on the needle.

Work squares 84–85 the same way. Fasten off.

Square 86 With WS facing, pick up and knit 25 sts across bottom edges of squares 74–71, then 24 more down right edges of squares 82 and 83. Complete large square. Leave last loop on the needle.

Square 87 With WS facing, pick up and knit 24 sts across bottom edge of square 86, and 24 more down right edges of squares 84 and 85. Complete large square. Fasten off.

Square 88 With WS facing, pick up and knit 7 sts across bottom edge of square 75, and 6 more down first 1"/2.5cm of right edge of square 86. Complete small square. Leave last loop on the needle.

Square 89 With WS facing, pick up and knit 6 sts across bottom edge of square 88, then 6 more sts down 2nd 1"/2.5cm of right edge of square 86. Complete small square. Leave last loop on the needle.

Work squares 90–95 the same way. Fasten off.

Work squares 96–99 same as 82–85.

Work Squares 100 and 101 same as 86 and 87.

Armhole triangle With RS facing, pick up and knit 13 sts up right edge of square 47. Complete triangle. Fasten off.

Neck edge triangle With RS facing, pick up and knit 7 sts down left edge of square 1. Complete triangle. Fasten off.

RIGHT FRONT/LEFT BACK

(make both pieces the same)

Work same as left front/right back panels, except face RS to pick up sts wherever instructed to face WS, and vice versa. This will change the direction of the slants. Also, pick up along a left edge where instructed to pick up along a right edge, and vice versa. This will create a mirror image of the other panels.

LARGE JACKET

LEFT FRONT/RIGHT BACK

(make both pieces the same)

Square 1 Follow small square pattern. Leave last loop on the needle.

Square 2 With RS facing, pick up and knit 6 sts up right edge of square 1, then cast on 6 more sts. Complete small square. Fasten off.

Square 3 Work same as square 1.

Squares 4–6 Work same as square 2, but leave last loop on the needle.

Square 7 With RS facing, pick up and knit 6 sts up right edge of square 6, and 6 more across bottom edge of square 1. Complete small square. Leave last loop on the needle. Work square 8 the same way. Fasten off.

Square 9 Cast on 7 sts, then with RS facing, pick up and knit 6 sts across bottom edge of square 3. Complete small square. Leave last loop on the needle.

Work squares 10–14 same as 7–8. Fasten off.

Work squares 15–20 same as 4–6.

Square 21 With RS facing, pick up and knit 13 sts up right edges of squares 14 and 8, and 12 more across bottom edges of squares 15 and 16. Complete medium square. Fasten off.

Square 22 Cast on 13 sts. With RS facing, pick up and knit 12 sts across bottom edges of squares 9 and 10. Complete medium square. Leave last loop on the needle.

Square 23 With RS facing, pick up and knit 12 sts up right edge of square 22, and 12 more across bottom edges of squares 11 and 12. Complete medium square. Leave last loop on

the needle.

Work squares 24 and 25 the same way. Fasten off.

Square 26 With RS facing, pick up and knit 25 sts up right edges of squares 21 and 25, and 24 more across bottom edges of squares 17–20. Complete large square. Fasten off.

Square 27 Cast on 25 sts. With RS facing, pick up and knit 24 sts across bottom edges of squares 22 and 23. Complete large square. Leave last loop on the needle.

Square 28 Work same as square 26, but leave last loop on the needle.

Square 29 Work same as square 28. Fasten off.

Square 30 Cast on 7 sts. With WS facing, pick up and knit 6 sts down right edge of square 20. Complete small square. Leave last loop on needle.

Square 31 With WS facing, pick up and knit 6 sts across bottom edge of square 30, and 6 more down first 1"/2.5cm of right edge of

square 26. Complete small square. Leave last loop on the needle.

Work squares 32–38 the same way. Fasten off.

Work squares 39–47 same as 30–38.

Square 48 Cast on 7 sts. With RS facing, pick up and knit 6 sts across first 1"/2.5cm of bottom edge of square 27. Complete small square. Leave last loop on the needle.

Square 49 With RS facing, pick up and knit 6 sts up right edge of square 48, and 6 more across 2nd 1"/2.5cm of bottom edge of square 27. Complete small square. Leave last loop on the needle.

Work squares 50–61 the same way. Fasten off.

Square 62 Cast on 13 sts. With WS facing, pick up and knit 12 sts down right edges of squares 39 and 40. Complete medium square. Leave last loop on the needle.

Square 63 With WS facing, pick up and knit 12 sts across bottom edge of square 62, and 12 more down right edges of squares 41 and 42.

Complete small square. Leave last loop on the needle.

Work squares 64–66 the same way. Fasten off.

Work squares 67–74 same as 22–25.

Work squares 75–78 same as 27–29.

Work squares 79–94 same as 48–61.

Work squares 95–102 same as 67–74.

Square 103 Cast on 25 sts. With WS facing, pick up and knit 24 sts down right edges of squares 62 and 63. Complete large square. Leave last loop on the needle.

Square 104 With WS facing, pick up and knit 24 sts across bottom edge of square 103, and 24 more down right edges of squares 64 and 65. Complete large square. Leave last loop on the needle.

Work square 105 the same way. Fasten off.

Square 106 Cast on 7 sts. With WS facing, pick up and knit 6 sts down first 1"/2.5cm of right edge of square 103. Complete small square. Leave last loop on the needle.

Square 107 With WS facing, pick up and knit 6 sts across bottom edge of square 107, and 6 more down 2nd 1"/2.5cm of right edge of square 103. Complete small square. Leave last loop on the needle.

Work squares 108–117 the same way. Fasten off.

Work squares 118–129 same as 39–47.

Work squares 130–135 same as 62–66.

Work squares 136–138 same as 103–105.

Armhole triangle With RS facing, pick up and knit 25 sts up right edge of square 78. Complete triangle. Fasten off.

Neck edge triangle With RS facing, pick up and knit 7 sts down left edge of square 1. Complete triangle. Fasten off.

RIGHT FRONT/LEFT BACK
(make both pieces the same)

Work same as left front/right back panels, except face RS to pick up sts wherever instructed to face WS, and vice versa. This will change the direction of the slants. Also, pick up along a left edge where instructed to pick up along a right edge, and vice versa. This will create a mirror image of the other panels.

FINISHING

Sew center back seam. Sew side and bottom sleeve seams.

Crochet 1 row in sc around each cuff edge, and around outer edge of entire jacket.

Crochet 10 more rows at neck edge, omitting 1 st at the end of each row.

Create 2 i-cords 18 (24)"/46 (61)cm in length using 2239, and sew around cuff edges.

Create an i-cord 98 (108)"/249 (274)cm in length using 2239, and sew around outer edge of jacket.

Create an i-cord 15"/38cm in length using P102. Sew to neck edge right below outer i-cord.

Create an i-cord 15"/38cm in length using 2239, and sew to base of back neck.

Sew buttons to front of jacket.

BLOCKING

Place jacket flat on a towel and pin to measurements. Spray with water and allow to dry. ◆

Small Size

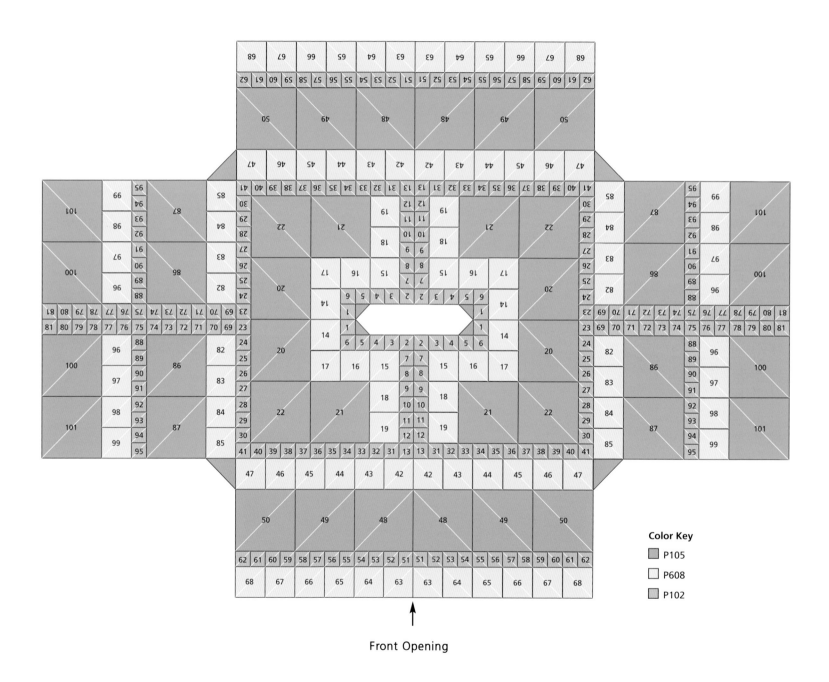

Color Key

■ P105

□ P608

■ P102

Front Opening

Large Size

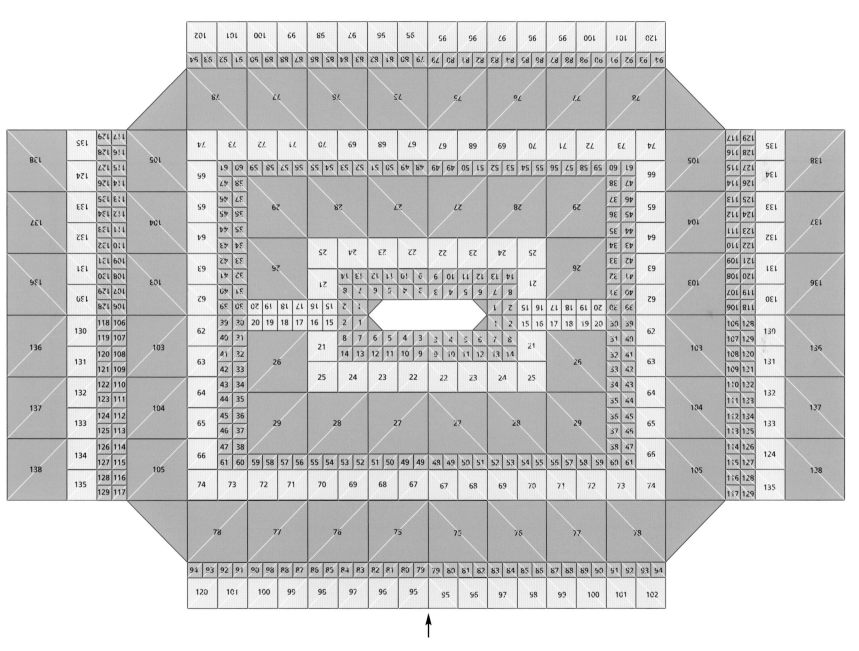

Front Opening

Wrap

easy

FINISHED MEASUREMENTS

◆ 20" x 80"/50cm x 204cm

MATERIALS

◆ 2 1.75oz/50g skeins of Koigu *Painter's Palette Premium Merino* (100% wool), 175yd/161m in each P217, P830, P513, P102, and P511D
◆ Size US 3 (3.25mm) circular needle (used as a straight needle), 60"/150cm long OR SIZE TO OBTAIN GAUGE
◆ Pins for blocking

GAUGE

28 stitches and 36 rows = 4" (10cm) in stockinette stitch.

TAKE TIME TO CHECK GAUGE.

Midnight Rapture Wrap, Top, and Skirt

The Midnight Rapture Skirt is a long, flared skirt in a drop-stitch pattern using five different colorways. One of the colors is used to make a sleeveless laced-front top. The wrap, which is knit sideways, completes the attractive outfit.

GARTER DROP STITCH PATTERN

Rows 1–4 Knit.

Row 5 K1, *yo twice, k1; rep from * to end.

Row 6 K1, *drop yos from needle, k1; rep from * to end.

Rep rows 1-6 for garter drop stitch pattern.

WRAP

Cast on 400 stitches using P217. Knit 2 rows. Begin working in garter drop stitch pattern, striping wrap as follows:

- Work pattern 3 times in P217
- 1 time in P830
- 1 time in P217
- 3 times in P830
- 1 time in P513
- 1 time in P830
- 3 times in P513
- 1 time in P102
- 1 time in P513
- 3 times in P102
- 1 time in P511D
- 1 time in P102
- 3 times in P511D

Knit 4 more rows, then bind off loosely.

BLOCKING

Place wrap flat on a towel, stretching widthwise to lengthen loops, and pin to measurements, placing pins about 1"/2.5cm apart on long edge to achieve a straight edge. Spray with water and allow to dry.

FRINGE

Fringes are 5 halved 8"/20.5cm strands. Make fringes of each color, and slip knot to matching color at wrap edge, at the garter st portion of the pattern. ◆

Skirt
beginner

FINISHED MEASUREMENTS

- Waist 25–30"/64–76cm
- Length 36"/92cm
- Hip 42"/106cm

MATERIALS

- 3 1.75oz/50g skeins of Koigu *Painter's Palette Premium Merino* (100% wool), 175yd/161m in each P217 and P830
- 1 skein in each P513, P102, and P511D
- Size US 3 (3.25mm) circular needle, 32"/81cm long OR SIZE TO OBTAIN GAUGE
- Size US 0 (2mm) circular needle, 24"/61cm long
- Sizes US 6 (4mm) and US 8 (5mm) circular needles, 40"/101.5cm long
- Waistband elastic about 1"/2.5cm wide, in length required for desired waist width
- Stitch marker

GAUGE

28 stitches and 36 rows = 4" (10cm) in stockinette stitch using size US 3 (3.25mm) needle.
TAKE TIME TO CHECK GAUGE.

SEED DROP STITCH PATTERNS

Pattern A

(use #8 needle)

Rnd 1 Purl.

Rnd 2 *P1, k1; rep from * to end.

Rnd 3 *K1, p1; rep from * to end.

Rnd 4 *P1, k1; rep from * to end.

Rnd 5 K1, *yo 4 times, k1; rep from * to end.

Rnd 6 K1, *drop yos from needle, k1; rep from * to end.

Pattern B

(use #6 needle)

Rnds 1–4 Work as pattern A.

Rnd 5 K1, *yo 3 times, k1; rep from * to end.

Rnd 6 K1, *drop yos from needle, k1; rep from * to end.

Pattern C

(use #3 needle)

Rnds 1–4 Work as pattern A.

Rnd 5 K1, *yo twice, k1; rep from * to end.

Rnd 6 K1, *drop yos from needle, k1; rep from * to end.

Pattern D

(use #0 needle)

Rows 1–4 Work as pattern A.

Row 5 K1, *yo once, k1; rep from * to end.

Row 6 K1, *drop yos from needle, k1; rep from * to end.

SKIRT

With #8 needle and P830, cast on 320 stitches. Join, taking care not to twist sts on needles. Place marker for beg of rnd and slip marker every rnd.

Begin working in seed drop stitch pattern, striping skirt as follows:

◆ Work 24 rnds pattern A, working 6 rnds each P830, P217, P513, P830. Change to #6 needle.

◆ Work 60 rnds pattern B, working 6 rnds each P217, P830, P513, P217, P830, P217, P102, P830, P513, P217. Change to #3 needle

◆ Work 60 rnds pattern C, working 6 rnds each P830, P513, P830, P217, P102, P830, P511D, P830, P217, P102. Change to #0 needle.

◆ Work 30 rnds pattern, working 6 rnds each P830, P217, P511D, P217, P830.

With P830 work 2"/5cm in stockinette stitch (knitting every round) for casing. Bind off all stitches. Fold 1"/2.5cm of casing to WS of skirt, leaving a small opening. Thread elastic through casing, adjust to desired waist width and sew opening closed.

BLOCKING

Place skirt flat on a towel, pulling lengthwise to straighten loops and pin to measurements, flaring out bottom edge of skirt as much as possible. Spray with water and allow to dry. ◆

Top

intermediate

FINISHED MEASUREMENTS

◆ Bust 38 (40)"/96 (102)cm

◆ Length 20 (21)"/50 (54)cm

MATERIALS

◆ 5 1.75oz/50g skeins of Koigu *Painter's Palette Premium Merino* (100% wool), 175yd/161m in P217

◆ Size US 0 (2mm) circular needle (used as a straight needle), 32"/81cm long OR SIZE TO OBTAIN GAUGE

◆ Size D/3 (3mm) crochet hook

◆ Stitch markers

◆ Stitch holders

GAUGE

32 stitches and 48 rows = 4" (10cm) in stockinette stitch.

TAKE TIME TO CHECK GAUGE.

GARTER DROP STITCH PATTERNS

Pattern A

Rows 1–4 Knit.

Row 5 K1, *yo twice, k1; rep from * to end.

Row 6 K1, *drop yos from needle, k1; rep from * to end.

Pattern B

Rows 1–4 Knit.

Row 5 K1, *yo once, k1; rep from * to end.

Row 6 K1, *drop yo from needle, k1; rep from * to end.

BODY

Cast on 200 (220) sts.

Work pattern A 3 times, then pattern B 3 times. Continue to alternate pats A and B in this manner until piece measures 12"/30cm from beg.

Divide for armhole

Place first and last 50 (55) sts on stitch holders for front panels. Cut yarn.

Center 100 (110) sts remain on the needle for back panel.

BACK

Attach new yarn to back panel.

Next 2 rows Bind off 5 sts at armhole edge, k to end—90 (100) sts.

Continue on back panel in pattern B only for 4"/10cm.

Place a marker on the needle at center back. Knit to marker, turn fabric, bind off 6 sts, knit to end. Continue working in pattern B, decreasing 1 st every other row at center back, until you have 10 sts left. Bind off 10 shoulder sts.

Attach yarn to remaining back panel sts at center back, bind off 6 sts, and work second half of back same as the first, reversing the shaping.

FRONTS

Work both front pieces the same:

Place sts from front stitch holder back onto the needle. Bind off 5 sts at armhole edge—45 (50) sts.

Work in pattern B for 3"/7.5cm.

Continue in pattern, decreasing 1 st at neck edge every other row until you have 10 sts left.

Work even until same length as back to shoulder. Bind off 10 shoulder sts.

Sew front shoulders to back shoulders.

EDGING

Work 2 rnds of sc around each armhole.

Work 5 rnds of sc along inner front edges.

Work 2 rnds of sc along neck edge, and across bottom edge.

Next rnd Working around edge of entire piece, *sc into each of the next 3 sc, ch3; rep from * around.

Cut three 1-yard/1-meter lengths of yarn and make into a simple braid. Thread braid through front crocheted edge loops to lace top together.

BLOCKING

Place top flat on a towel and pin to measurements. Spray with water and allow to dry. ◆

Vest

intermediate

FINISHED MEASUREMENTS

◆ Bust 42"/ 106cm

◆ Length 19.5"/ 50cm

MATERIALS

◆ 3 1.75oz/50g skeins of Koigu *Painter's Palette Premium Merino* (100% wool), 175yd/161m in each P416L, and P446

◆ Size US 3 (3.25mm) needles OR SIZE TO OBTAIN GAUGE

◆ Size D/3 (3mm) crochet hook, or size to correspond with needle

GAUGE

28 stitches and 36 rows = 4" (10cm) in stockinette stitch.

TAKE TIME TO CHECK GAUGE.

TECHNIQUES

See Stitch Workshop for:

◆ Practice square

◆ Triangles

◆ Joining seams with 2 needles and a crochet hook

Note Join all panels with P446 using 2 needles and a crochet hook.

Patchwork Vest and Pants

Combat the cold weather with style. The idea for the Patchwork Pants came to Maie many years ago. They are made from alternating mitred squares of seed stitch and garter stitch. A diamond and triangle vest with crochet around it complements the pants.

LARGE DIAMOND PATTERN

Cast on, or pick up and knit, 49 sts using P416L.

Row 1 Sl 1 purlwise, k to center st, p1, k to last st, p1.

Row 2 Sl 1 purlwise, k to center 3 sts, SK2P, k to last st, p1.

Rep these 2 rows until you have 3 sts left.

Next row K3tog.

Cut yarn, and slide tail through remaining loop.

SMALL DIAMOND PATTERN

Cast on, or pick up and knit, 25 sts using P446, then work same as large diamond.

LARGE TRIANGLE PATTERN

Pick up and knit 25 sts using P446.

Row 1 Sl 1 purlwise, k to last 3 sts, k2tog, p1.

Row 2 Sl 1 purlwise, k to last st, p1.

Rep these 2 rows until you have 3 sts left.

Next row K2tog.

Cut yarn, and slide tail through remaining loop.

SMALL TRIANGLE PATTERN

Pick up and knit 13 sts using P416L, then work same as large triangle.

VEST

LARGE PANELS

(make 2)

Work a large diamond.

Pick up and knit 25 sts along top right edge of diamond, and work a large triangle.

Pick up and knit 25 sts along top left edge of diamond, and work a large triangle beginning with row 2 (this will reverse the direction of the triangle).

Pick up and knit 25 sts along inner edge of right hand triangle, and 24 more along the inner edge of left hand triangle, and work another large diamond.

Continue in this manner until you have a total of 7 large diamonds and 12 large triangles.

CENTER BACK PANELS

(make 2)

Work a small diamond.

Pick up and knit 13 sts along top right edge of diamond, and work a small triangle.

Pick up and knit 13 sts along top left edge of diamond, and work a small triangle, beginning with row 2 (this will reverse the direction of the triangle).

Continue in this manner until you have a total of 5 small diamonds and 10 small triangles.

With RS facing and P446, pick up and knit 13 sts along inner edge of right hand triangle, and 12 more along the inner edge of left hand triangle. Work a triangle as follows:

Row 1 (WS) K to center st, p1, k to last st, p1.

Row 2 Sl 1, SKP, k to center 3 sts, SK2P, k to last 3 sts, k2tog, p1.

Rep these 2 rows until you have 5 sts left.

Next row K1, SK2P, k1

Cut yarn, and slide tail through remaining 3 sts.

Join the two center back panels lengthwise.

Join outer edges of center back to bottom 2.5 triangles of large panels.

RIGHT ARMHOLE PANEL

Work a small diamond.

Pick up and knit 13 sts along top right edge of diamond, and work a small triangle.

Pick up and knit 13 sts along top left edge of diamond, and work a small triangle beginning with row 2.

Pick up and knit 13 sts along inner edge of

right hand triangle, and 12 more along the inner edge of left hand triangle, and work another small diamond.

Continue in this manner until you have a total of 3 small diamonds and 4 small triangles.

Work 5th triangle as foll: Pick up and knit 13 sts along top left edge of diamond, and work a small triangle beginning with row 2.

Join left edge to bottom one and a half triangles of right hand large panel. Fold large panel over at shoulder. Join right edge of armhole panel to top triangle of large panel.

LEFT ARMHOLE PANEL

Work same as right armhole panel, working 5th

triangle as foll: Pick up and knit 13 sts along top right edge of diamond, and work a small triangle.

Join right edge to bottom 1.5 triangles of left hand large panel. Fold large panel over at shoulder. Join left edge of armhole panel to top triangle of large panel.

RIGHT FRONT PANEL

Work same as Right Armhole Panel, making 4 small diamonds and 6 small triangles. Work a 7th triangle same as the 5th triangle.

LEFT FRONT PANEL

Work same as Left Armhole Panel, making 4

small diamonds and 6 small triangles. Work a 7th triangle same as the 5th triangle.

FINISHING

With RS facing and P446, work 2 rows of sc around outer edge of entire vest, and around each armhole.

BLOCKING

Place vest flat on a towel and pin to measurements. Spray with water and allow to dry. ◆

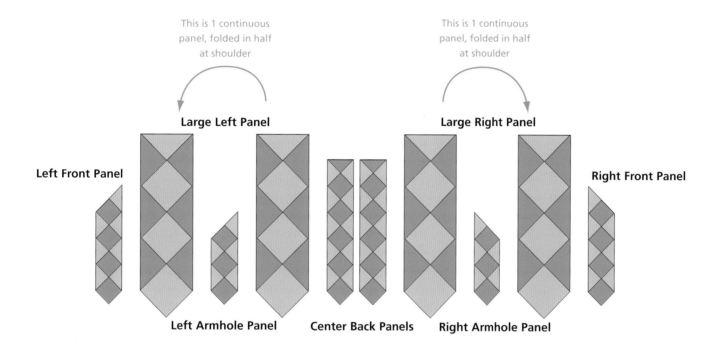

This is 1 continuous panel, folded in half at shoulder

This is 1 continuous panel, folded in half at shoulder

Large Left Panel

Large Right Panel

Left Front Panel

Right Front Panel

Left Armhole Panel

Center Back Panels

Right Armhole Panel

Pants

experienced

FINISHED MEASUREMENTS

◆ Hip 40"/101.5cm

◆ Length 45"/114cm

MATERIALS

◆ 2 1.75oz/50g skeins (each approx 175yd/161m) of Koigu *Painter's Palette Premium Merino* (wool) in # P446 (A), #P416L (B), #P409 (D), #P450 (E) and #P439 (F)

◆ 3 skeins in # P436 (C)

◆ 30"/76.5cm of ½"/1.5cm elastic

◆ Tapestry needle

◆ Two size 3 (3.25mm) dpn

◆ Circular needle size 3 (3.35mm)

GAUGE

45-st square = 4" (10cm) over garter stitch using size 3 (3.25mm) needles.

TAKE TIME TO CHECK GAUGE.

Notes

1 All the squares begin with 45 sts. They are knit alternately in garter stitch and seed stitch using two dpn.

2 The colors of the squares are shown on the graph. The direction of the decreases up the center of squares are shown on the schematic.

SQUARE 1

Cast on 45 sts. Work in garter st as foll:

Row 1 (WS) Work 44 sts, p1.

Row 2 (RS) Sl 1, work 20 sts, SK2P, work 20 sts, p1—43 sts.

Row 3 Sl 1, work 20 sts, p1, work 20 sts, p1.

Row 4 Sl 1, work 19 sts, SK2P, work 19 sts, p1—41 sts.

Rep rows 3 and 4, working 1 less st before and after the center dec, until 3 sts rem, ending with a RS row.

Last row (WS) SK2P.

Cut yarn leaving 1½"/4cm and pull it through last loop.

SQUARE 2

Cast on 22 sts, pick up and k 23 along side edge of first square—45 sts.

Beg with row 1, and working in seed st, complete as for first square.

SQUARE 3

Cast on 22 sts, pick up and k 23 sts along side edge of 2nd square—45 sts.

Beg with row 1, complete as for first square.

SQUARE 4

Pick up and k 23 sts along side edge of 3rd square, cast on 22 sts—45 sts.

Beg with row 1, and working in seed st, complete as for first square.

First row of squares have been completed.

SQUARE 5

Cast on 22 sts, pick up and k 23 sts along top of square 1—45 sts.

Beg with row 1, and working in seed st, complete as for first square.

SQUARE 6

Pick up and k 23 sts along top of square 2, 22 sts along side of square 5—45 sts.

Beg with row 1, complete as for first square.

SQUARE 7

Pick up and k 22 sts along top of square 3, 23 sts along side of square 6—45 sts.

Beg with row 1, and working in seed st, complete as for first square.

SQUARE 8

Cast on 22 sts, pick up and k 23 sts along top of square 4—45 sts while working the square 8, pick up 1 st every other row from square 7 (see Stitch Workshop).

Beg with row 1, complete as for first square.

Cont in this way until 8 rows of 4 squares have been worked, or desired length of leg to crotch. Work 2nd half of pants in same way, foll diagrams for color and direction of decreases.

INNER LEG GUSSETS

With RS facing, circular needle and C, pick up and k 88 sts along sides of the top 4 squares. P 1 row on WS.

Next row (RS) K 77, turn, p to end.

Next row (RS) K 66, turn, p to end. Cont in this way to work 11 sts less at end of every RS row 4 times more. Place all sts on a holder. Work in same way along other side of leg. Join the leg sides tog with 2 needles and a crochet hook.

Note With the extra width created at the crotch, extra squares are created at center front and back.

WAIST SQUARES

Cont making squares, alternating seed st and garter st and foll diagrams for color and direction of decreases.

WAIST

Pick up sts at waist with circular needle. Work in garter st with C for 2"/5cm at front of pants and with short rows continue knitting at back of pants until center back measures 4"/10cm Bind off. Turn edge of band to inside. Sew to inside 1"/2.5cm wide. Make six 1½"/4cm i-cords for belt tabs. Sew belt tabs to pant band. Make braided belt 40"/101.5cm long as shown on diagram and pull through tabs. ◆

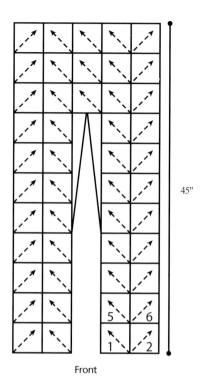

Direction of Decreases

45"

Front

40"

13"

32"

Back

Color Placement Diagram

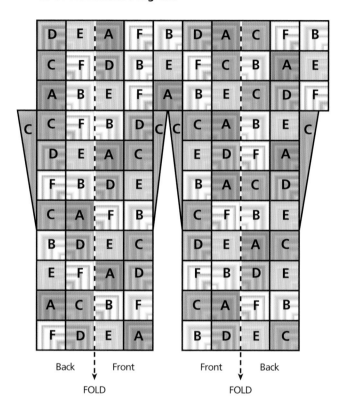

D	E	A	F	B	D	A	C	F	B
C	F	D	B	E	F	C	B	A	E
A	B	E	F	A	B	E	C	D	F

Back   Front   Front   Back

FOLD   FOLD

Braided Belt

Color Key

A = P446	D = P409
B = P416L	E = P450
C = P436	F = P439

Keepsake Shawl

intermediate

The Keepsake Shawl is a large square, beginning with many stitches and ending with just 3. Its shape makes it work equally well as a throw. Maie's original shawl, a true heirloom, was made from leftover Koigu yarns.

FINISHED MEASUREMENTS

◆ 60 x 60"/152 x 152cm

MATERIALS

◆ 1 1.75oz/50g skein of Koigu *Painter's Palette Premium Merino* (100% wool), 175yd/161m in each P612, P816, P511L, P814, P605, P608, P621, P513, P602, P628, P623, and P324

◆ Size US 6 (4mm) 40"/100cm circular needle (used as straight needles) OR SIZE TO OBTAIN GAUGE

◆ Size G/6 (4mm) crochet hook or size to correspond with needle

◆ Stitch marker

GAUGE

24 stitches and 30 rows = 4" (10cm) in stockinette stitch.

TAKE TIME TO CHECK GAUGE.

LACE PATTERN

(Multiple of 9 sts plus 1)

Row 1 (RS) K1, *yo, SKP, k4, k2tog, yo, k1; rep from * to end

Row 2 K1, *k1, p6, k2; rep from * to end

Row 3 K1, *k1, yo, SKP, k2, k2tog, yo, k2; rep from * to end

Row 4 K1, *k2, p4, k3; rep from * to end

Row 5 K1, *k2, yo, SKP, k2tog, yo, k3; rep from * to end

Row 6 K1, *k3, p2, k4; rep from * to end

Rep these 6 rows for pattern.

STRIPE SEQUENCE

[2 rows P816, 2 rows P612] twice.

12 rows P816

[2 rows P511L, 2 rows P816] twice.

12 rows P511L

[2 rows P814, 2 rows P511L] twice.

12 rows P814

[2 rows P605, 2 rows P814] twice.

12 rows P605

[2 rows P608, 2 rows P605] twice.

12 rows P608

[2 rows P621, 2 rows P608] twice.

12 rows P621

[2 rows P513, 2 rows P621] twice.

12 rows P513

[2 rows P602, 2 rows P513] twice.

12 rows P602

[2 rows P628, 2 rows P602] twice.

12 rows P628

[2 rows P623, 2 rows P628] twice.

12 rows P623

[2 rows P324, 2 rows P623] twice.

12 rows P324

Continue color sequence from the beginning to the end of the shawl.

SHAWL

Cast on 399 sts using P612. Mark center st.
Work 2 rows in garter st.
Rows 1 and 2 Work in lace pattern to center st, k center st, then work in lace pattern again (as if from beg of row) to last st.
Continue as shown in chart, decreasing 1 st on either side of center st on every RS row.
After 14 rows, begin stripe sequence. When you have 3 sts left, cut yarn, and slide tail through remaining 3 sts.
Work 1 row in sc around entire shawl.

BLOCKING

Soak shawl in warm water and pin to maximum size. Allow to dry.

FRINGE

Fringes are 6 halved 12"/30.5cm strands of mixed colors. Attach fringes every 2"/5cm around outer edge of shawl. ◆

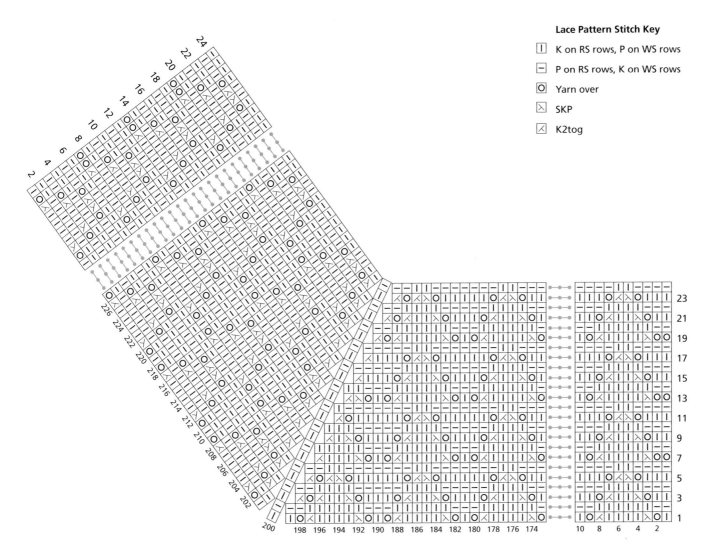

Lace Pattern Stitch Key

☐	K on RS rows, P on WS rows
▬	P on RS rows, K on WS rows
Ⓞ	Yarn over
◩	SKP
◪	K2tog

KNITTED MEASUREMENTS

◆ Bust 50"/127cm

◆ Length 34"/86cm

◆ Sleeve (neck to wrist) 29"/74cm

MATERIALS

◆ 8 1.75oz/50g skeins of Koigu *Painter's Palette Premium Merino* (100% wool), each 175yd/161m in P716

◆ Size US 6 (4mm) circular needle (used as straight needles), 40"/100cm long OR SIZE TO OBTAIN GAUGE

◆ Stitch markers

GAUGE

24 stitches and 30 rows = 4" (10cm) in stockinette stitch.

TAKE TIME TO CHECK GAUGE.

Floppy Jacket

intermediate

This jacket is easy flowing with a loose drape. It is quick and easy to knit—a comfortable garment that can be worn year-round.

DROP STITCH PATTERN

(any number of sts)

Row 1 (RS) K1, *yo, k1; rep from * to end.

Row 2 K1, *drop yo from needle, k1; rep from * to end.

Rep these 2 rows for pattern.

EDGE PATTERN

(even number of sts)

Row 1 (WS) Knit.

Row 2 (RS) K1, *yo, k2tog tbl; rep from * to last st, k1.

Row 3 Knit.

Row 4 and 6 Knit.

Row 5 (WS) Rep row 2.

Rows 7–9 Rep rows 1–3.

BODY

Cast on 200 sts loosely, and knit 2 rows.

Work in edge pattern for 9 rows.

Knit 1 row.

Work in drop stitch pattern for 106 rows (53 reps).

Divide for armhole

Place first and last 45 sts on stitch holders for front panels. Cut yarn.

Center 110 sts remain on the needle for back panel.

BACK

Attach new yarn to sts on needle.

Shape armhole

Row 1 (RS) Bind off 10 sts, work in drop stitch pattern to last 10 sts, k10.

Row 2 Bind off 10 sts, work in pattern to end of row.

Continue in pattern for 40 more rows (20 reps).

Shape neck and shoulders

Next row (RS) Work in pattern across 30 sts, join 2nd ball of yarn and bind off center 30 sts, then work in pattern across remaining 30 sts.

Work 9 more rows evenly in pattern across each shoulder, then bind off all sts.

FRONTS (work both the same)

Place sts from front stitch holder back onto the needle, and work in drop stitch pattern for a total of 50 rows (25 reps), decreasing 1 st at neck edge every 3rd row 15 times (30 sts).

Bind off all sts.

SLEEVES

Cast on 40 sts loosely, and knit 2 rows.

Work in edge pattern for 21 rows , ending with row 3.

Knit 1 row.

Work in drop stitch pattern for a total of 70 rows (45 reps), increasing 1 st at each end of row every 4th row 15 times (70 sts).

Bind off all sts.

EDGING

Sew shoulder seams.

With RS facing, pick up and knit 100 sts up right front edge, 30 sts across neck edge, and 100 sts down left front edge (230 sts).

Knit 1 row, then work first 3 rows of edge pattern.

Knit 2 rows, then bind off all sts.

FINISHING

Sew side and sleeve seams. Set in sleeves.

BLOCKING

Place jacket flat on a towel and pin to measurements, pulling loops lengthwise.

Spray with warm water and allow to dry. ◆

Magique Cloak
experienced

Many knitting designers have tackled the cube; Maie felt the modular technique was perfect for it. In the Magique Cloak, the cubes are knit separately and then joined. The elevated join lines give the cloak a vibrant stained-glass effect.

KNITTED MEASUREMENTS

- Bust 48 (56, 64, 72)"/122 (142, 162, 182)cm
- Length 41"/104cm (all sizes)

MATERIALS

- 5 skeins KPM 2170 (solid color)
- 3 1.75oz/50g skeins of Koigu *Painter's Palette Premium Merino* (100% wool), 175yd/161m each P609, P405, P134, P419, P217, P439, and P608D
- 2 skeins each P524, P124, P123, and P818
- 1 skein each P105D, P121, P112, P518, P212, P211 and P819
- Size US 3 (3.25mm) needles OR SIZE TO OBTAIN GAUGE
- Size D/3 (3mm) crochet hook, or size to correspond with needle

GAUGE

28 stitches and 36 rows = 4" (10cm) in stockinette stitch.

TAKE TIME TO CHECK GAUGE.

Note Knit all sts in this garment through the back loop.

TECHNIQUES

See Stitch Workshop for:

- Practice square
- Triangles
- Joining seams with 2 needles and a crochet hook

SIMPLE CUBE PATTERN

Large Diamond 1

Cast on 41 sts.

Row 1 WS Sl 1 purlwise, k to to last st, p1.

Row 2 Sl 1 purlwise, k to center 3 sts, SK2P, k to last st, p1.

Rep these 2 rows until you have 3 sts left.

Next row K3tog.

Cut yarn, and slide tail through remaining loop.

Triangle 2

Turn large diamond upside down (place cast on row at top).

With RS facing, pick up and knit 11 sts along 1st half of right hand side of cast on row.

Row 1 WS Sl 1 p wise, k to last st, p1.

Row 2 SKP, k to last st, p1.

Rep these 2 rows until you have 2 sts left.

Next row K2tog.

Leave last loop on the needle.

Small diamond 3

With RS facing, pick up and knit 10 sts along left edge of triangle, and 10 more along 2nd half of right side of cast on row.

Work same as large diamond, leave last loop on the needle.

Triangle 4

With RS facing, pick up and knit 10 sts along left edge of small diamond.

Row 1 WS SKP, k to last st, p1.

Row 2 Sl 1 purlwise, k to last st, p1.

Rep these 2 rows until you have 2 sts left.

Next row K2tog.

Cut yarn, and slide tail through remaining loop.

Triangle 5

With RS facing, pick up and knit 11 sts along 2nd half of left hand side of cast on row.

Work as small triangle 4, leave last loop on the needle.

Small Diamond 6

With WS facing, pick up and knit 10 sts along right edge of triangle, and 10 more along 1st half of left hand side of cast on row.

Work same as large diamond, beginning with row 2. Leave last loop on the needle.

Triangle 7

With WS facing, pick up and knit 10 sts along right edge of small diamond.

Row 1 RS SKP, k to end.

Row 2 K to last st, k last st together with corresponding edge st of triangle 4.

Rep these 2 rows until you have 2 sts left.

Next row K2tog.

Cut yarn, and slide tail through remaining loop.

COMPLEX CUBE PATTERN

Diamond 1 Cast on 21 sts.

Row 1 WS Sl 1 purlwise, k to to last st, p1.

Row 2 Sl 1 purlwise, k to center 3 sts, SK2P, k to last st, p1.

Rep these 2 rows until you have 3 sts left.

Next row K3tog.

Cut yarn, and slide tail through remaining loop.

Diamond 2

Turn diamond 1 upside down.

Cast on 11 sts, then with RS facing, pick up and knit 10 more sts along right half of cast on row of diamond 1.

Work same as diamond 1. Leave last loop on the needle.

Diamond 3

With RS facing, pick up and knit 10 sts along left half of cast on row of diamond 1, then cast on 11 more sts.

Work same as diamond 1.

Diamond 4

With RS facing, pick up and knit 10 sts along left edge of diamond 2, and 11 more along right edge of diamond 3.

Work same as diamond 1.

Triangle 5

Turn work upside down.

With RS facing, pick up and knit 11 sts along cast on edge of diamond 3.

Row 1 WS Sl 1 purlwise, k to last st, p1.

Row 2 SKP, k to last st, p1.

Rep these 2 rows until you have 2 sts left.

Next row K2tog.

Leave last loop on the needle.

Diamond 6

With RS facing, pick up and knit 10 sts along left edge of triangle 5, and 11 more along right edge of diamond 1.

Work same as diamond 1. Leave last loop on the needle.

Triangle 7

With RS facing, pick up and knit 10 sts along left edge of diamond 6.

Row 1 WS SKP, k to last st, p1.

Row 2 Sl 1 p wise, k to last st, p1.

Rep these 2 rows until you have 2 sts left.

Next row K2tog.

Cut yarn, and slide tail through remaining loop.

Triangle 8

With RS facing, pick up and knit 11 sts along cast on edge of diamond 2.

Work same as triangle 7. Leave last loop on the needle.

Diamond 9

With WS facing, pick up and knit 11 sts along right right side of triangle 8, and 10 more along left half of cast on row of diamond 1.

Work same as diamond 1, beginning with row 2. Leave last loop on the needle.

Triangle 10

With WS facing, pick up and knit 10 sts along right edge diamond 9.

Row 1 RS SKP, k to last st, p1.

Row 2 K to last st, k last st together with corresponding edge st of triangle 7.

Rep these 2 rows until you have 2 sts left.

Next row K2tog.

Cut yarn, and slide tail through remaining loop.

LEFT HALF CUBE PATTERN

Large Triangle 1

Cast on 21 sts.

Row 1 RS SKP, k to last st, p1.

Row 2 Sl 1 purlwise, to last st, p1.

Rep these 2 rows until you have 2 sts left.

Next row K2tog.

Cut yarn, and slide tail through remaining loop.

Work pieces 2–4 same as simple cube pattern.

RIGHT HALF CUBE PATTERN

Large Triangle 1

Cast on 21 sts.

Row 1 WS SKP, k to last st, p1.

Row 2 Sl 1 purlwise, k to last st, p1.

Rep these 2 rows until you have 2 sts left.

Next row K2tog.

Cut yarn, and slide tail through remaining loop.
Work pieces 2–4 same as 5–7 of simple cube
pattern.

EDGE TRIANGLE PATTERN

Cast on 41 sts.

Row 1 WS Knit.

Row 2 SKP, k to center 3 sts, SK2P, k to last 3 sts,
k2tog, p1.

Rep these 2 rows until you have 5 sts left.

Next row Sl 1, SK2P, k1.

Cut yarn, and slide tail through remaining 3 sts.

CLOAK

Make simple and complex cubes, half cubes and
edge triangles following the diagram. Work the
smallest size inside the brown outlines, the next
larger size inside the green outlines, the next
larger size inside the orange outlines and the
largest size using the entire diagram. With KPM
2170, join together, using 2 needles and crochet
hook, following the diagram for placement.

FRONT BAND

Cast on 33 sts using KPM 2170.

Row 1 RS K1, * sl 1 purlwise with yarn in front,
k1; rep from * to end.

Row 2 K1, p1, * sl 1 purlwise with yarn in back,
p1; rep from * to last st, k1.

Repeat these 2 rows until front band measures
92"/233.5cm, then bind off all sts.

Sew band around front edge of cloak.

BLOCKING

Place cloak flat on towel, folding front band in
half lengthwise. Spray with water, and allow
to dry. ◆

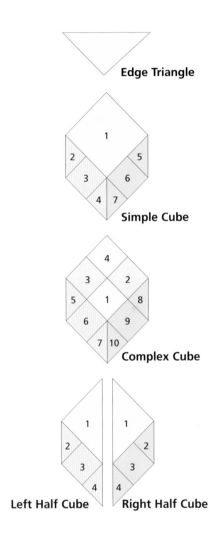

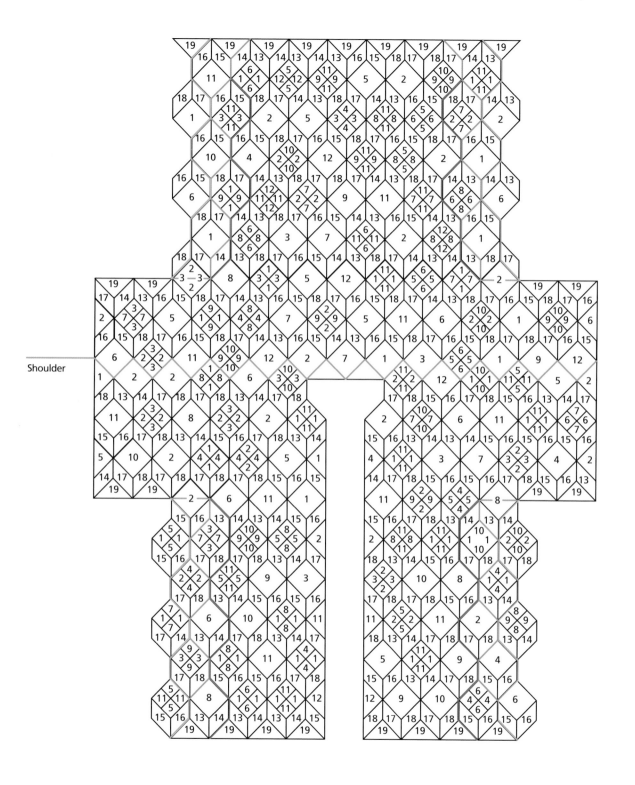

Main Diamonds:
1 - P524
2 - P608D
3 - P105D
4 - P121
5 - P124
6 - P123
7 - P112
8 - P518
9 - P212
10 - P211
11 - P818
12 - P819

Sides:
13 - P609
14 - P405
15 - P134
16 - P419
17 - P217
18 - P439

Edge Triangles:
19 - KPM 2170

Shoulder

KNITTED MEASUREMENTS

◆ Hip 51"/129.5cm

◆ Bust 40"/101.5cm

◆ Length 53"/134.5cm

◆ Upper arm 20"/50.5cm

MATERIALS

◆ 4 1.75oz/50g skeins (each approx 175yd/161m) of Koigu *Painter's Palette Premium Merino* (wool) each in #P822 and #P823L

◆ 3 skeins each in #P805, #P612, #P511L, #P814 and #P837

◆ 2 each in #P816L, #P831L, #P511D, #P823D, #P851 and #P816D

◆ 2 1.75oz/50g skeins of Koigu *Premium Merino* (wool) in #2239 (for joining panels)

◆ Different lengths size 3 (3.25mm) dpns to suit size of shape to be knit or size 3 (3.25mm) circular needles OR SIZE TO OBTAIN GAUGE

◆ Size C/2 (2.75mm) crochet hook

◆ Stitch markers

GAUGE

25 sts = 1.75"/4.5cm over garter st square using size 3 (3.25mm) needles.

TAKE TIME TO CHECK GAUGE.

Robe-Diamond Dress
experienced

This creation uses fourteen hand-dyed colorways. It took many sheets of graph paper before Maie found the large diamond design she was looking for. The variations in shapes, direction of decreases, combination of stitch patterns and interplay of color make this an exciting project to work on.

TECHNIQUES

See Stitch Workshop for:

- Practice square
- Diamond
- Triangles
- Joining seams with 2 needles and a crochet hook

Ridge Pattern

8-row pat *4 rows garter st, 4 rows St st; rep from * (8 rows) for ridge pat.

OR

12-row pat *6 rows garter st, 6 rows St st; rep from * (12 rows) for ridge pat.

Note Some squares are made with the 8-row pat, some are made with the 12-row pat and some are made with different combinations of garter st and St st, for example, 6 rows garter st with 4 rows St st. For ease in writing this instruction, we just refer to the ridge pat. Any combination of garter st and St st can be used without changing the basic look of the garment.

Seed Stitch

Row 1 *K1, p1; rep from * to end.
Row 2 K the purl sts and p the knit sts.
Rep row 2 for seed st.

CENTER PANEL #1

(make 2)

A. Large center diamond

K-cast on 258 sts. Work in ridge pat and color sequence (see below) as foll:

Row 1 (WS) K257, p1.
Row 2 (RS) Sl 1, k63 tbl, SKP, k62 tbl, SKP, k62 tbl, SKP, k63 tbl, p1—255 sts.
Row 3 Sl 1, k63 tbl, p1, k62 tbl, p1, k62 tbl, p1, k63 tbl, p1.
Row 4 Sl 1, k2tog, k60 tbl, SK2P, k60 tbl, SK2P, k60 tbl, SK2P, k60 tbl, SKP, p1—247 sts.
Row 5 Sl 1, p1, k60 tbl, p1, k60 tbl, p1, k60 tbl, p1, k60 tbl, p2.

Rep rows 4 and 5, working dec as established every RS row (therefore, 8 sts are dec'd every other row), and keeping to ridge pat, until 7 sts rem. Cut yarn, draw through these 7 sts and pull tog. Sew open side tog.

A. Color sequence in large diamond

4 rows each P822; P511D; P511L; P823L; P814; P823D; P612; P805; P851; P816L; P831L; P837; P511D; P511L; P814.

C1 (RS)

K-cast on 33 sts; pick up and k 32 sts along RS of large diamond A from right corner to center of diamond—65 sts. Work in seed st in foll color sequence: 15 rows P612; 10 rows P823L; 15 rows P814; 15 rows P511L; work with P81451 to end of square.

Work decs as foll:

Row 1 (WS) Work 64 sts in seed st, p1.
Row 2 (RS) Sl 1, work 30 sts seed st, SK2P, work 30 sts seed st, p1.
Row 3 Sl 1, work 30 sts seed st, p1, work 30 sts seed st, p1.
Row 4 Sl 1, work 29 sts seed st, SK2P, work 29 sts seed st, p1.

Rep rows 3 and 4, dec 2 sts in the center every RS row, until 3 sts rem, ending with RS row.

Last row (WS) SK2P.

Cut yarn leaving 1½"/4cm and pull it through last loop.

C1 (LS)

Pick up and k 32 sts beg at center of large diamond A to left corner; L-cast on 33 sts—65 sts. Work seed st, color sequence and decs same as C1 (RS) square.

D1 (RS)

Pick up and k 33 sts along C1 (RS) and 32 sts along large diamond A to top corner—65 sts. Work in seed st in foll color sequence: 10 rows

P814; 10 rows P511L; 10 rows P814; 15 rows P823L, work with P61251 to end of square. Work decs same as C1 (RS) square.

D1 (LS)

Pick up and k 32 sts along top left of large diamond A and 33 sts along C1 (LS)—65 sts. Work seed st, color sequence and decs same as D1 (RS).

E1 (RS)

Pick up 32 sts along diamond A side from center to right corner, L-cast on 33 sts—65 sts. Work in seed st in foll color sequence: 15 rows P816D; 10 rows P851; 10 rows P816L; 10 rows P831; work with P83751 to end of square. Work decs same as C1 (RS) square.

E1 (LS)

K-cast on 33 sts, pick up and k 32 sts along left corner of diamond A to center of diamond A—65 sts. Work seed st, color sequence and decs same as E1 (RS).

F1 (RS)

Pick up and k 32 sts along diamond A and 33 sts along E1 (RS). Work in seed st in foll color sequence: 10 rows P831; 10 rows P837; 10 rows P816L; 15 rows P851; work with P816D to end of square.

F1 (LS)

Pick up and k 33 sts along E1 (LS) and 32 sts along diamond A. Work seed st, color sequence and decs same as F1 (RS).

G (RS)—half square

Pick up and k 33 sts along side of E1 (RS) and 32 sts from side of C1 (RS)—65 sts. Work in ridge pat and color sequence (see following page) as foll:

Row 1 (WS) K tbl to last st, p1.

Row 2 (RS) Sl 1, k2tog, p28, SK2P, p28, SKP, p1.

Row 3 Sl 1, k61 tbl, p1.

Rep rows 2 and 3, working 2 less sts between decs every RS row, until there are 5 sts on

needle. Cut yarn and draw through these sts, pull tog and weave in end.

Color sequence for G1 (RS) 4 rows each P822; P511D; P511L; P823L; then work with P814 to end of half square.

G (LS)

Pick up and k 33 sts along side of C1 (LS) and 32 sts from E1 (LS)—65 sts. Work ridge pat, color sequence and decs same as G (RS).

H—half square

Pick up 33 sts from F1 (LS) and 32 sts along F1 (RS)—65 sts. Work in ridge pat and color sequence as foll: 4 rows P837; 4 rows P831; 4 rows P851; 4 rows P816L; work with P612 to end of half square. Work decs same as G (RS) K1 (RS-top corner) left angle triangle

Pick up and k 32 sts along D1 (RS). Work in garter st and color sequence (see below) and work as foll:

Row 1 (WS) K31 tbl, p1.

Row 2 (RS) Sl 1, knit tbl to last 3 sts, k2tog, p1.

Row 3 Sl 1, knit tbl to last st, p1.

Rep rows 2 and 3 until 3 sts rem, ending with RS row.

Next row (WS) SK2P.

Last row K1, cut yarn and pull through st.

Color sequence for K1 (RS) *4 rows each P805, P822, P823L; rep from *.

Note Carry colors not in use along side of triangle to avoid weaving in ends later.

K2 (RS-top corner) right angle triangle

Pick up and k 33 sts along C1 (RS). Work in garter st and color sequence (see below) and join to K1 triangle as foll:

Row 1 (WS) K31 tbl, p1.

Row 2 (RS) Sl 1, SKP, knit tbl to last st, sl last st to RH needle, with LH needle, pick up 1 st along side of K1 triangle, sl last st from K2 triangle to LH needle and p these 2 sts tog.

Row 3 Sl 1, knit tbl to last st, p1.

Rep rows 2 and 3 until 3 sts rem, ending with RS row.

Next row (WS) SK2P.

Last row K1, cut yarn and pull through st.

Color sequence for K2 (RS) *4 rows each P805; P823L; P822; rep from *.

Note Carry colors not in use along side of triangle to avoid weaving in ends later.

Work K1 and K2 triangles along bottom right corner in same way. For top and bottom left corners, beg with K2 triangle, then work K1 triangle and pick up along K2 to join triangles. When center panel 1 is completed, make 2nd panel for back.

CENTER PANEL #2

(make 2)

B. Large center diamond

K-cast on 194 sts. Work in ridge pat and color sequence (see below) as foll:

Row 1 (WS) K193, p1.

Row 2 (RS) Sl 1, k47 tbl, SKP, k46 tbl, SKP, k46 tbl, SKP, k47 tbl, p1—191 sts.

Row 3 Sl 1, k47 tbl, p1, k46 tbl, p1, k46 tbl, p1, k47 tbl, p1.

Row 4 Sl 1, k2tog, k44 tbl, SK2P, k44 tbl, SK2P, k44 tbl, SK2P, k44 tbl, SKP, p1—183 sts.

Row 5 Sl 1, p1, k44 tbl, p1, k44 tbl, p1, k44 tbl, p1, k44 tbl, p2.

Rep rows 4 and 5, working dec as established every RS row (therefore, 8 sts are dec'd every other row), and keeping to ridge pat, until 7 sts rem. Cut yarn, draw through these 7 sts and pull tog. Sew open side tog.

Color sequence in large diamond

6 rows each P837; P831; P816L; P805; P851; P823D; P814; P511D; work with P511L end of square.

O1 (RS)

K-cast on 16 sts, pick up and k 17 sts along B—

33 sts. Work in garter st and color sequence as foll: *4 rows each P823D; P823L; rep from *. Work decs same as C1 (RS), working row 2 as foll: Sl 1, work 14 sts, SK2P, work 14 sts, p1.

P1 (RS)

Pick up 17 sts along side of O1 and 16 sts along B—33 sts. Work in garter st and color sequences as foll: *4 rows each P805; P816L; rep from * to end. Work decs same as O1 square.

O2 (RS)

Pick up 17 sts along side of P1 and 16 sts along B to top corner—33 sts. Work in garter st and color sequences as foll: *4 rows each P823D; P823L; rep from * to end. Work decs same as O1 square.

O1 (LS)

Pick up and k 17 along B, L-cast on 14 sts—33 sts. Complete same as O1 (RS) square.

P1 (LS)

Pick up 17 sts along B, 16 sts along O1. Complete same as P1 (RS) square.

O2 (LS)

Pick up 17 sts along side of B and 16 sts along side of P1. Complete same as O2 (RS) square.

P2 (RS)

Pick up 17 sts along side of B, L-cast on 16 sts. Complete same as P1 (RS) square.

O3 (RS)

Pick up 17 sts along side of B and 16 sts along P2. Complete same as O1 (RS)

P3 (RS)

Pick up 17 sts along side of B and 16 sts along O3. Complete same as P1 (RS).

P2 (LS)

K-cast on 16 sts, pick up and k 17 along B—33 sts. Complete same as P1 (RS).

O3 (LS)

Pick up 17 sts along side of P2 and 16 sts along

B—33 sts. Complete same as O2 RS square.

P3 (LS)

Pick up 17 sts along side of O3 and 16 sts along B—33 sts. Complete same as P1 RS square.

O4

Pick up 17 sts along P3 (LS) and 16 sts from P3 (RS)—33 sts. Work in garter st, colors and decs same as O1 (RS).

C1 (RS)

K-cast on 32 sts, pick up 33 sts along squares O1 and P1 (RS)—65 sts. Work in seed st and color sequence as foll: 15 rows P612; 10 rows P823L; 15 rows P814; work with P814 to end of square. Work decs same as C1 (RS) on center panel #1.

C1 (LS)

Pick up 33 sts along squares P1 and O1 (LS), L-cast on 32 sts, Work in seed st and color sequence as foll: 15 rows P612; 10 rows P823L; 15 rows P814; work with P814 to end of square.

Work decs same as C1 (RS).

P4 (RS)

Pick up 16 sts along C1 (RS) and 17 sts along O2 (RS). Work in garter st and complete same as P1 (RS).

O5 (RS)

Pick up 16 sts along C1 (RS) and 17 sts along P4 (RS). Work in garter st and complete same as O1 (RS).

P4 (LS)

Pick up 17 sts along O2 (LS) and 16 sts along C1 (LS). Work in garter st and complete same as P1 (RS).

O5 (LS)

Pick up 17 sts along P4 (LS) and 16 sts along C1 (LS). Work in garter st and complete same as O1 (RS).

C2 (RS)

Pick up 33 sts along squares O3 and P2 (RS), L-cast on 32 sts—65 sts. Complete same as C1 (RS).

C2 (LS)

K-cast on 32 sts, pick up 33 sts along squares P2 and O3 (LS)—65 sts. Complete same as C1 (LS).

H (RS)

Pick up 33 sts along squares O4 and P3 (RS) and 32 sts along C2 (RS)—65 sts. Work in ridge pat and color sequence as foll: 4 rows each P837, P831, P851, P816L, work with P612 to end of piece. Work decs same as G (RS) on first panel.

H (LS)

Pick up 32sts along C2 (LS), 33 sts along P3 and O4 (LS)—65 sts. Complete same as H (RS).

J1

Pick up 8 sts from P4 (RS) and 16 sts from O2 (RS), pick up 17 sts from O2 and 8 sts from P4 (LS)—49 sts. Work in ridge pat and color sequence as foll: 4 rows each P837, P816L, P816D, P831, P612, P823, P511D, work with and

P511L to end of piece. Work decs same as C1 (RS) on panel #1, working row 2 as foll: Sl 1, work 22 sts, SK2P, work 22 sts, p1.

J2 (RS)

Pick up 8 sts along C2 (RS), 16 sts along P2 (RS), 17 sts along O1 (RS) and 8 sts along C1 (RS)—49 sts. Work in ridge pat, color sequence and decs same as J1.

J3 (LS)

Pick up 8 sts along C1 (LS), 16 sts along O1 (LS), 16 sts along P2 (LS) and 8 sts along C2 (LS)—49 sts. Work in ridge pat, color sequence and decs same as J1.

G1 (RS)

Pick up 24 sts along C2 (RS) and 25 sts along J2 (RS)—49 sts. Work in ridge pat in foll color sequence: 4 rows each P822, P511D, P511L, P823L, work with P814 to end of piece. Work decs same as G (RS) on panel #1, working row 2 as foll: Sl 1, k2tog tbl, k20 tbl, SK2P, k20 tbl, SKP, p1.

G2 (RS)

Pick up 24 sts along J2 (RS) and 25 sts along C1 (RS)—49 sts. Complete same as G1 (RS).

G1 (LS)

Pick up 24 sts along J3 (LS) and 25 sts along C2 (LS)—49 sts. Complete same as G1 (RS).

G2 (LS)

Pick up 24 sts along C1 (LS) and 25 sts along J3(LS)—49 sts. Complete same as G1 (RS).

L1 (RS)

Pick up 33 sts along C1 (RS) side and 16 along O5 (RS)—49 sts. Work in ridge pat in foll color sequence: *4 rows each P822, P805, P823L; rep from *. Work decs as foll:

Row 1 (WS) Sl 1, work to last st, p1.

Row 2 Sl 1, k2tog, work to last 3 sts, SKP, p1. Rep rows 1 and 2 until 5 sts rem.

Next row (RS) K2tog, k1, SKP. Work 1 row even. Last row SK2P. Fasten off last st.

L1 (LS)

Pick up 16 sts along O5 (LS) and 33 sts along C1 (LS)—49 sts. Complete same as L1 (RS).

L2 (RS)

Pick up 33 sts along C2 (RS). Complete same as L1 (RS).

L2 (LS)

Pick up 33 sts along C2 (LS). Complete same as L1 (RS).

CENTER PANEL #3

(make 2)

A. Large center diamond

Work same as large center diamond (A) on Panel #1.

C1 (RS) and (LS)

Work same as panel #1.

E (RS) and (LS)

Work same as panel #1.

G (RS) and (LS)

Work same as panel #1.

I (RS)

Pick up 33 sts along C1 (RS) and 32 sts along A—65 sts. Work in ridge pat in foll color sequence: 4 rows each P823D, P823L, P816D, P513, work with P814 to end of piece. Work decs same as G (RS) on panel #1.

I (LS)

Pick up 33 sts along A (RS) and 32 sts along C1 (LS)—65 sts. Complete same as I (RS).

Work the other two I's at lower edge to correspond.

L (4 corners)

Pick up 33 sts along C1 (RS) and complete same as L1 (RS) on panel #2. Work other 3 corners to correspond.

PANEL #4—SLEEVES

(make 4)

Make center diamond (B) same as Panel # 2.

M1 (RS)

K-cast on 24 sts and pick up 25 sts along B—49 sts. Work in seed st in foll color sequence: P511D on first half of square, P823D on 2nd half of square. Work decs same as J1 (RS) on panel #2.

M2 (RS)

K-cast on 24 sts and pick up 25 sts along B—49 sts. Work in seed st in foll color sequence: P823L on first half of square, P823D on 2nd half of square. Complete same as M1.

N1 (RS)

Pick up 25 sts along M1 (RS) and 24 sts along B—49 sts. Work in seed st in foll color sequence: P612 on first half of square, P805 on 2nd half of square. Complete same as M1.

N2 (RS)

Pick up 25 sts along side of M2 (RS) and 24 sts along B—49 sts. Work in seed st in foll color sequence: P851 on first half of square, P805 on 2nd half of square. Complete same as M1.

M1 (LS)

Pick up 25 sts along B and L-cast on K 24 sts—49 sts. Work in seed st in foll color sequence: P511D on first half of square, P823D on 2nd half of square. Complete same as M1.

N1 (LS)

Pick up 25 sts along B and 24 sts along M1 (LS) —49 sts. Work in seed st in foll color sequence: P612 on first half of square, P805 on 2nd half of square. Complete same as M1.

M2 (LS)

K-cast on 24 sts and pick up 25 sts along B—49 sts. Work in seed st in foll color sequence: P823L on first half of square, P823D on 2nd half of square. Complete same as M1.

N2 (LS)

Pick up 24 sts along M2 (LS) and 25 sts along B—49 sts. Work in seed st in foll color sequence: P851 on first half of square, P805 on 2nd half of square. Complete same as M1.

J1

Pick up 25 sts along N1 (RS) and 24 sts along side of N1 (LS). Complete same as J1 on panel #2.

J2

Pick up 25 sts along N2 (LS) and 24 sts along N2 (RS). Complete same as J1.

G1 (RS)

Pick up 25 sts along M2 (RS) and 24 sts along M1 (RS). Complete same as G1 on panel #2.

G1 (LS)

Pick up 25 sts along M1 (LS) and 24 sts along side of M2 (LS). Complete same as G1 on panel #2.

K1 (RS)

Pick up 12 sts along N1 (RS) and 25 sts along J1—37 sts. Work in ridge pat and color sequence as foll: 4 rows each P822, P816L, P822, P831, P822, P851, P822, P816D, P822, P612, P822, P511D, P822, P814, P822, P511L, work with P822 to end of triangle. Work decs same as K1 (RS) on panel #1.

K2 (RS)

Pick up 25 sts along M1 and 12 sts along N1 (RS). Work in ridge pat and color sequence as foll: 4 rows each P816L, P822, P831, P822, P851, P822, P816D, P822, P612, P822, P511D, P822, P814, P822, P511L, work with P822 to end of triangle. Work decs and join to K1 same as panel #1.

Work rem 3 corners to correspond.

Pick up 93 sts along the lower edge of panel 1 with circular needle or long straight needle, and k 1 row with color #2239. Pick up 93 sts along the top edge of panel 2 and knit 1 row with #2239. With WS of panel #1 and panel #2 facing, use crochet hook to join the 2 panels (see Stitch Workshop).

Work in same way to join panel #2 and #3. Join center panel #1 and sleeve panel #4 in the same way. Join other sleeve to center panel #1 on the other side.

Work in same way to join the panels on the back of the garment. Join shoulder and sleeve panels by picking up 103 sts from back and 103 sts along front. Join sleeve seams by picking up 70 sts from one sleeve edge and 70 sts from the other sleeve.

Join the garment sides by picking up 93 sts along panel #2 front to panel #2 back. In order to give extra width around the hip, work garter st for 3 rows along both sides before joining. Repeat the same for other side. The sides remain open for panels 3, leaving this as slits.

FINISHING

Weave any loose ends to the back of garment with crochet hook or tapestry needle.

BLOCKING

Place dress flat on towel and pin to measurements. Spray with water and allow to dry. ◆

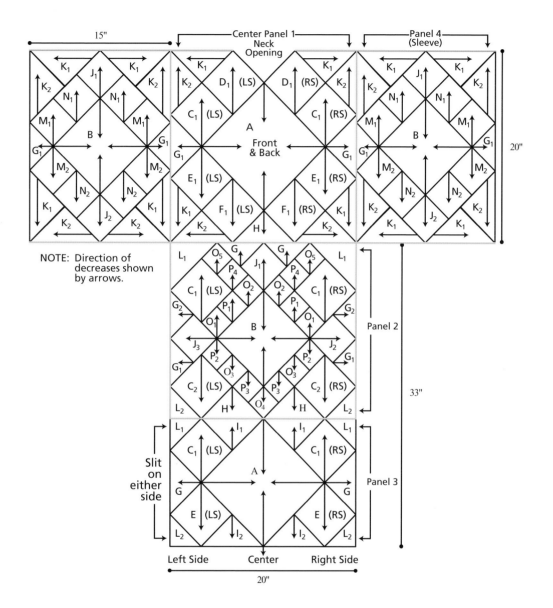

15"

Center Panel 1
Neck Opening

Panel 4 (Sleeve)

K_1 J_1 K_1 K_2 N_1 N_1 M_1 K_1 K_2 D_1 (LS) D_1 (RS) K_2 K_1 K_1 J_1 K_1

K_2 N_1 N_1 M_1 B G_1 M_1 M_2 N_2 N_2

C_1 (LS) A Front & Back C_1 (RS)

G_1 M_2 M_2 G_1

E_1 (LS) E_1 (RS)

K_1 N_2 N_2 K_1 K_2 J_2 K_2

K_1 F_1 (LS) F_1 (RS) K_1 K_2 H K_2

K_2 N_1 N_1 M_1 B G_1 M_2 N_2 N_2 K_2 J_2 K_2 K_1

20"

NOTE: Direction of decreases shown by arrows.

L_1 O_5 G G O_5 L_1

C_1 (LS) P_4 P_4 C_1 (RS)
J_1
O_2 O_2
G_2 P_1 P_1 G_2
O_1 B O_1
J_3 J_2
G_1 P_2 P_2 G_1
C_2 (LS) O_3 O_3 C_2 (RS)
P_3 P_3
L_2 H O_4 H L_2

Panel 2

33"

L_1 I_1 I_1 L_1

C_1 (LS) C_1 (RS)

Slit on either side

A

G G

E (LS) E (RS)

L_2 I_2 I_2 L_2

Panel 3

Left Side   Center   Right Side

20"

KNITTED MEASUREMENTS

◆ Width 40"/102cm
◆ Length 30"/76cm

MATERIALS

◆ 1 1.75oz/50g skein of *Koigu Painter's Palette Premium Merino* (100% wool), 175yd/161m in each P511D, P105D, P142, P513, P111, P121, P818, P810, P136, and P419
◆ Size US 4 (3.5mm) needles OR SIZE TO OBTAIN GAUGE
◆ Size E/4 (3.5mm) crochet hook, or size to correspond with needle
◆ Stitch markers

GAUGE

25 stitches and 32 rows = 4" (10cm) in stockinette stitch.
TAKE TIME TO CHECK GAUGE.

TECHNIQUES

See Stitch Workshop for:

◆ Practice square
◆ Triangles
◆ Half square
◆ Joining seams using 2 needles and a crochet hook

Butterfly Poncho
intermediate

This cheerful modular poncho, knit in the square with a textured knit-and-purl pattern, calls for ten different colors. Use the suggested color palette or choose your own. It can be worn as shown on the model, or as shown on p.111.

COLOR SEQUENCE

For each piece, choose 6 of the first 9 colors listed.

Work 8 rows in each color in any order of your choice, then begin sequence again.

SQUARE PATTERN

(make 6)

Cast on 144 sts. Place a stitch marker at center of needle.

Row 1 WS P3, *k3, p3; rep from * to last 3 sts before marker, p3, slip marker, p3, ** k3, p3; rep from ** to end.

Row 2 K the knits and p the purls to last 3 sts before marker, k2tog, k1, slip marker, k1, SKP, k the knits and p the purls to end.

Row 3 K the knits and p the purls to last 3 sts before marker, p3, slip marker, p3, k the knits and p the purls to end

Row 4 As row 2.

Row 5 P the knits and k the purls to last 3 sts before marker, p3, slip marker, p3, p the knits and k the purls to end.

Row 6 As row 2.

Row 7 As row 3.

Row 8 As row 2.

Row 9 As row 3.

Rep rows 2–9 only until you have 6 sts left.

Next 4 rows:

Row 1 WS Purl.

Row 2 K2tog, k2, SKP.

Row 3 Purl

Row 4 K2tog, SKP

Cut yarn, and slide tail through remaining 2 loops.

RIGHT SHOULDER TRIANGLE PATTERN

(make 1)

Cast on 72 sts.

Row 1 WS P3, *k3, p3; rep from * to last 3 sts, p3.

Row 2 K1, SKP, k the knits and p the purls to end.

Row 3 K the knits and p the purls to last 3 sts, p3.

Row 4 As row 2.

Row 5 P the knits and k the purls to last 3 sts, p3.

Row 6 As row 2.

Row 7 As row 3.

Row 8 As row 2.

Row 9 As row 3.

Rep rows 2–9 only until you have 3 sts left.

Next row K1, SKP.

Cut yarn, and slide tail through remaining 2 loops.

LEFT SHOULDER TRIANGLE PATTERN

(make 1)

Cast on 72 sts.

Row 1 WS P6, *k3, p3; rep from * to end.

Row 2 K the knits and p the purls to last 3 sts, k2tog, k1.

Row 3 P3, k the knits and p the purls to end.

Row 4 As row 2.

Row 5 P3, p the knits and k the purls to end.

Row 6 As row 2.

Row 7 As row 3.

Row 8 As row 2.

Row 9 As row 3.

Rep rows 2–9 only until you have 3 sts left.

Next row, k1, SKP.

Cut yarn and slide tail through remaining loops

NECK HALF SQUARES

(make 2)

Cast on 144 sts.

Row 1 WS P3, *k3, p3; rep from * to last 3 sts before marker, p3, slip marker, p3, **k3, p3; rep from ** to end.

Row 2 SKP, k the knits and p the purls to last 3 sts before marker, k2tog, k1, slip marker, k1, SKP, k the knits and p the purls to last 2 sts, k2tog.

Row 3 K the knits and p the purls to last 3 sts before marker, p3, slip marker, p3, k the knits and p the purls to end

Row 4 As row 2.

Row 5 P1, p the knits and k the purls to last 3 sts before marker, p3, slip marker, p3, p the knits and k the purls to last st, p1.

Row 6 As row 2.

Row 7 As row 3.

Row 8 As row 2.

Row 9 As row 3.

Rep rows 2–9 only until you have 8 sts left.

Next 3 rows

Row 1 RS K2tog 4 times (4 sts)

Row 2 Purl

Row 3 K2tog twice (2 sts)

Cut yarn, and slide tail through remaining 2 sts.

JOINING PIECES

Join half squares at neck, leaving 8" neck opening. Using P419, pick up and knit 72 sts along edge of center square and work 2 rows in garter st. Work the same on corresponding edge to be joined, then join pieces using 2 needles and a crochet hook.

GARTER EDGING

Using P419, pick up and knit 288 sts along edges of square pieces only at front of poncho. Work 2 rows in garter st, then bind off all sts. Work same edging for back.

BLOCKING

Wet poncho in warm water, lay flat, pin to measurements, and allow to dry. ◆

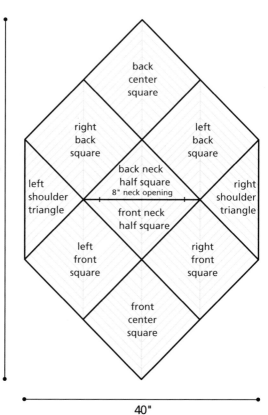

KNITTED MEASUREMENTS

◆ Bust 47"/119cm
◆ Length 32"/82cm

MATERIALS

◆ 3 1.75oz/50g skeins of Koigu *Painter's Palette Premium Merino* (100% wool), 175yd/161m in each P513 and P121
◆ 2 skeins in P413
◆ 3 1.75oz/50g skeins of Koigu *Premium Merino* (100% wool), 175yd/161m in each 2405 and 2400
◆ Size US 3 (3.25mm) needles OR SIZE TO OBTAIN GAUGE
◆ Size D/3 (3mm) crochet hook, or size to correspond with needle

GAUGE

28 stitches and 36 rows = 4" (10cm) in stockinette stitch.
TAKE TIME TO CHECK GAUGE.

TECHNIQUES

This tunic is made in one piece with only two shoulder seams (see diagram).
See stitch workshop for:

◆ Practice square
◆ Triangles
◆ Knitting a square in two different colors

Joker Tunic
experienced

This sleeveless tunic is knit in the domino or mitered square technique: different-sized squares are knit together diagonally so they appear as diamond shapes. The diamond shapes form the hem, which is finished with whimsical tassels. The joy of modular knitting is that there are few seams.

SIMPLE DIAMOND PATTERN A

Cast on, or pick up and knit, 49 sts using P513.

Row 1 (WS) Sl 1 p wise, k to last st, p1.

Row 2 Sl 1 p wise, k to center 3 sts, SK2P, k to last st, p1.

Rep rows 1 and 2 rows twice more.

Row 7 Sl 1 p wise, p to end.

Row 8 Sl 1 p wise, k to center 3 sts, SK2P, k to last st, p1.

Rep rows 7 and 8 twice more.

Rep these 12 rows until you have 3 sts left.

Next row SK2P.

Cut yarn, and slide tail through remaining loop.

SIMPLE DIAMOND PATTERN B

Cast on, or pick up and knit, 49 sts using P121.

Row 1 (WS) Sl 1 p wise, k to last st, p1.

Row 2 Sl 1 p wise, k to center 3 sts, SK2P, k to last st, p1.

Rep rows 1 and 2 rows 4 more times.

Row 11 Sl 1 p wise, p to end.

Row 12 Sl 1 p wise, k to center 3 sts, SK2P, k to last st, p1.

Rep rows 11 and 12 twice more.

Rep these 16 rows until you have 3 sts left.

Next row SK2P.

Cut yarn, and slide tail through remaining loop.

COMPLEX DIAMOND PATTERN

Small diamond 1 Using 2405, pick up 7 sts from simple diamond A and 6 sts from simple diamond B.

Row 1 (WS) Sl 1 p wise, k to last st, p1.

Row 2 Sl 1 p wise, k to center 3 sts, SK2P, k to last st, p1.

Rep these 2 rows until you have 3 sts left.

Next row SK2P.

Leave last loop on the needle.

Small diamond 2 Using 2405, with RS facing, pick up and knit 7 sts down top left edge of previous diamond, then cast on, or pick up and knit, 6 sts (13 sts). Work diamond same as diamond 1.

Cut yarn, and slide tail through remaining loop after diamond 4.

Small diamonds 3 and 4 Using 2400, work the same as small diamond 2.

Small diamond 5 Using 2405, pick up and knit 7 sts from small diamond 1, then with RS facing, pick up 6 more sts from top right edge of simple diamond A or B. Work same as small diamond 1. Cut yarn, and slide tail through remaining loop.

Small diamond 6 Using 2405, pick up and knit 7 sts from small diamond 5, then with RS facing,

pick up 6 more sts from top right edge of simple diamond A or B. Work same as small diamond 1. Cut yarn, and slide tail through remaining loop.

Small diamond 7 Using 2405, work the same as small diamond 6.

Medium diamond 8 Using P413 and with RS facing, pick up and knit 13 sts down top left edges of diamonds 6 and 5, and 12 more sts up top left edges of diamonds 2 and 3.

Row (WS) Sl 1 p wise, k to last st, p1.

Row 2 Sl 1 p wise, k to center 3 sts, SK2P, k to last st, p1.

Rows 3 and 5 Sl 1 p wise, purl to end.

Rows 4 and 6 As row 2.

Row 7 As row 1.

Row 8 Switch to 2400, Sl 1 p wise, k to center 3 sts, SK2P, k to last st, p1.

Row 9 As row 1.

Row 10 Switch back to P413, Sl 1 p wise, k to center 3 sts, SK2P, k to last st, p1.

Row 11 As row 1.

Rows 12, 14 and 16 As row 2.

Rows 13 and 15 As row 3.

Rows 17, 19, 21 and 23 As row 1.

Rows 18, 20 and 22 As row 2.

Row 24 SK2P.

Cut yarn, and slide tail through remaining st.

Small diamond 9 Using 2400, pick up and knit 7 sts along small diamond 7, then with RS facing, pick up and knit 6 sts from top right edge of medium diamond 8. Work diamond same as diamond 1.

Small diamond 10 With RS facing, pick up and knit 7 sts down top left edge of previous diamond, and 6 more sts up top right edge of medium diamond 8. Work same as diamond 1.

Small diamond 11 Using 2400 and with RS facing, pick up and knit 7 sts down 2nd half of top left edge of medium diamond 8, then pick up and knit 6 more sts up top right edge of diamond 4. Work diamond same as diamond 1.

Small diamond 12 Using 2400 and with WS facing, pick up and knit 7 sts down top right edge of diamond 11, and 6 more sts up remaining top left edge of medium diamond 8. Work diamond same as diamond 1.

Small diamond 13 Using 2400 and with WS facing, pick up and knit 7 sts down top right edge of diamond 12, and 6 more sts up top left edge of diamond 10. Work diamond same as diamond 1. Cut yarn, and slide tail through remaining loop.

RIGHT EDGE TRIANGLE PATTERN

Triangle 1 Using 2405, Cast on, or pick up and knit, 7 sts.

Row 1 (WS) Sl 1 p wise, k to last st, p1.

Row 2 Sl 1, SKP, k to last st, p1.

Rep these 2 rows until you have 2 sts left.

Next row SKP.

Leave last loop on the needle.

Diamonds 2–4 Work same as in complex diamond pattern.

Triangle 5 Using P413 and with RS facing, pick up and knit 13 sts up top left edges of diamonds 2 and 3.

Row 1 (WS) Sl 1 p wise, k to last st, p1.

Row 2 Sl 1 SKP, k to last st, p1.

Rows 3 and 5 Sl 1 p wise, purl to end.

Rows 4 and 6 As row 2.

Row 7 As row 1.

Row 8 Switch to 2400, sl 1, SKP, k to the last st, p1.

Row 9 As row 1.

Row 10 Switch back to P413, sl 1, SKP, k to last st, p1.

Row 11 As row 1.

Rows 12, 14 and 16 As row 2.

Rows 13 and 15 As row 3.

Rows 17, 19, 21 and 23 As row 1.

Rows 18, 20 and 22 As row 2.

Row 24 K2tog.

Cut yarn, and slide tail through remaining st.

Diamonds 6 and 7 Work same as diamonds 11 and 12 in complex diamond pattern.

Triangle 8 With WS facing, pick up and knit 7 sts down top right edge of diamond 7. Knit 1 row, then work triangle same as triangle 1. Cut yarn, and slide tail through remaining loop.

LEFT EDGE TRIANGLE PATTERN

Triangle 1 Using 2405, cast on, or pick up and knit 7 sts.

Row 1 (WS) Sl 1 p wise, k to last st, p1.

Row 2 Sl 1 p wise, k to last 3 sts, k2tog, p1.

Rep these 2 rows until you have 2 sts left.

Next row K2tog.

Leave last loop on the needle.

Diamonds 2 and 3 Work same as diamonds 5 and 6 in complex diamond pattern.

Triangle 4 Using P413 and with RS facing, pick up and knit 13 sts down top left edges of diamonds 2 and 3.

Row 1 (WS) Sl 1 p wise, k to last st, p1.

Row 2 Sl 1 p wise, k to last 3 sts, k2tog, p1.

Rows 3 and 5 Sl 1 p wise, purl to end.

Rows 4 and 6 As row 2.

Row 7 As row 1.

Row 8 Switch to 2400, Sl 1 p wise, k to last 3 sts, k2tog, p1.

Row 9 As row 1.

Row 10 Switch back to P413, Sl 1 p wise, k to last 3 sts, k2tog, p1.

Row 11 As row 1.

Rows 12, 14 and 16 As row 2.

Rows 13 and 15 As row 3.

Rows 17, 19, 21 and 23 As row 1.

Rows 18, 20 and 22 As row 2.

Row 24 K2tog.

Cut yarn, and slide tail through remaining st.

Diamonds 5–7 Work same as diamonds 8–10 in complex diamond pattern.

Triangle 8 With RS facing, pick up and knit 7 sts down top left edge of diamond 7. Work triangle same as triangle 1. Cut yarn, and slide tail through remaining loop.

ARMHOLE TRIANGLE PATTERN

Diamonds 1–3 Work same as in complex diamond pattern.

Triangle 4 Using 2400, with RS facing, pick up and knit 7 sts down top right edge of diamond 3. Work same as triangle 1 left edge triangle pattern.

Diamonds 5 and 6 Work same as in complex diamond pattern. Leave last loop on the needle.

Triangle 7 With WS facing, pick up and knit 7 sts down top right edge of diamond 6, then pick up and knit 6 more sts. Knit 1 row, then work triangle same as triangle 4.

Triangle 8 With RS facing, pick up and knit 7 sts down top left edge of diamond 3,then cast on 6 more sts.

Row 1 (WS) Sl 1 p wise, k to last st, p1.

Row 2 Sl1, SKP, k to center 3 sts, SK2P, k to last 3 sts, k2tog, p1.

Row 3 As row 1.

Row 4 As row 2.

Row 5 As row 1.

Row 6 Sl 1, SK2P, p1.

Row 7 As row 1.

Row 8 SK2P.

Cut yarn, and slide tail through remaining loop.

TUNIC

The tunic is made of twelve rows (see diagram). Each row below the armholes includes ten shapes, either simple diamonds or complex diamonds.

Row I Work 10 separate simple diamonds, 5 following pattern A, and 5 following pattern B. Turn diamonds upside down, with cast on edge at the top, in alternating order as shown on chart.

Row II Work 10 complex diamonds, picking up sts from top edges of diamonds of row 1.

Row III Work 10 simple diamonds, alternating patterns same as row 1, and picking up sts from top edges of diamonds of row 2. Cast on sts for right edge of rightmost diamond.

Rows IV and VI As row 2.

Rows V and VII As row 3.

Row VIII Work 8 complex diamonds in pattern at center of row. Work armhole triangles at armholes.

Row IX Work 6 simple diamonds in pattern as on graph.

Row X Work 4 complex diamonds in pattern as on graph. Work an edge triangle at each row edge, picking up sts from outer diamonds of previous row.

Row XI (begin shoulders) Work 4 simple diamonds in pattern, omitting center diamond-neck and picking up from edge triangles and diamonds of previous row.

Row XII Work 4 edge triangles at each shoulder, picking up from diamonds of previous row.

FINISHING

Join shoulders.

Work 1 row in sc using P121 around bottom edge.

Using 2400, work 3 rows in sc around each armhole, skipping every 3rd st to make armhole smaller. Work 5 rows in sc around neck edge.

Place 1 fringe (10 doubled 6"/15.5cm strands of P513) at the tip of each bottommost diamond.

BLOCKING

Place tunic flat on a towel and pin to measurements. Spray with water and allow to dry. ◆

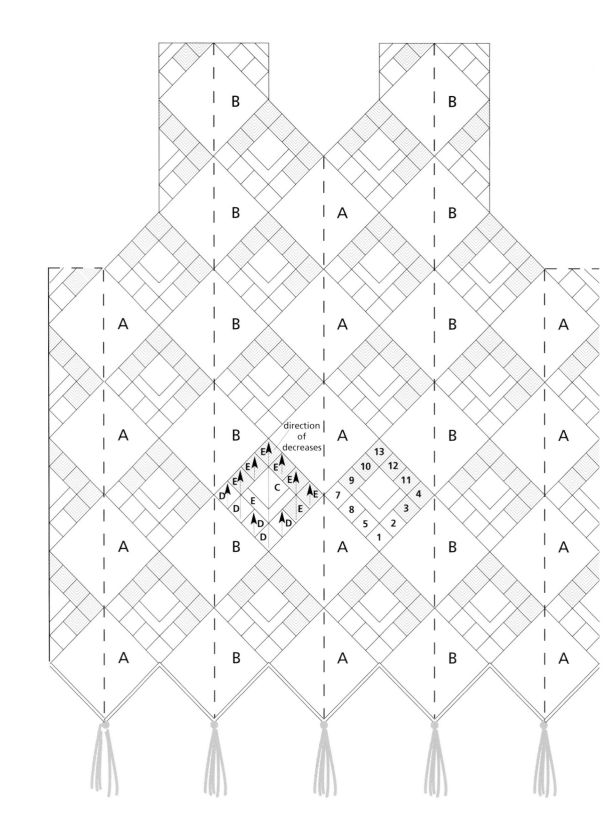

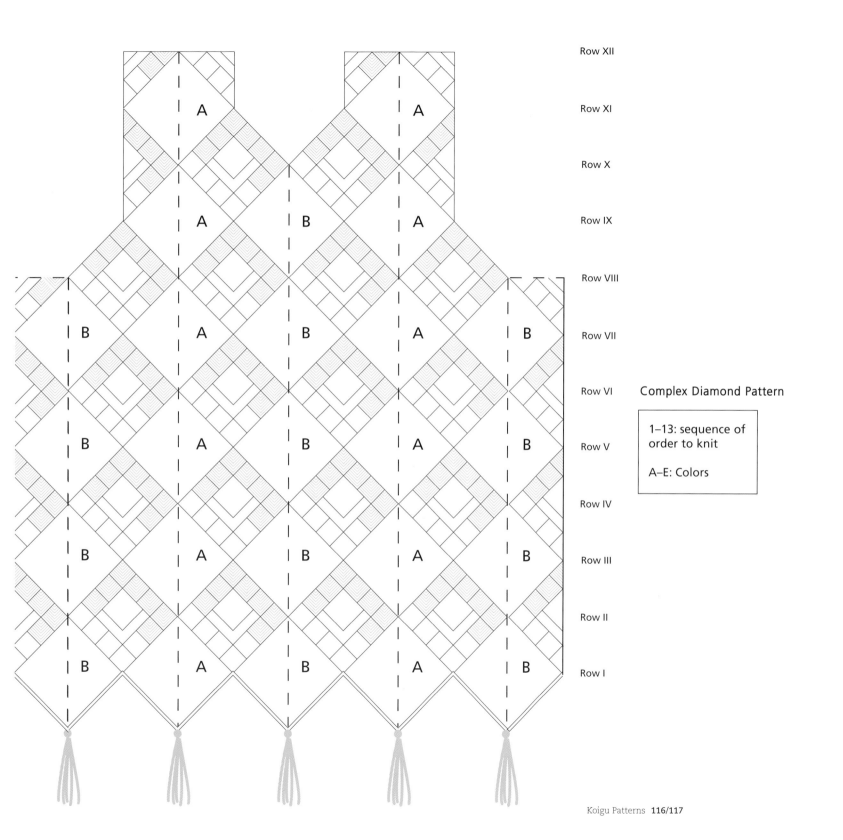

Row XII

Row XI   A   A

Row X

Row IX   A   B   A

Row VIII

Row VII   B   A   B   A   B

Row VI

Row V   B   A   B   A   B

Row IV

Row III   B   A   B   A   B

Row II

Row I   B   A   B   A   B

Complex Diamond Pattern

1–13: sequence of order to knit

A–E: Colors

Oriental Jacket
experienced

The Oriental Jacket, designed in 1998, is a Koigu classic—a loose-fitting jacket composed of squares in three different sizes with random color distribution. The squares are knit to each other horizontally and vertically, using two solid and six variegated colors.

KNITTED MEASUREMENTS

- Bust 48"/122cm
- Length 33"/84cm

MATERIALS

- 3 1.75oz/50g skeins of Koigu *Painter's Palette Premium Merino* (100% wool), 175yd/161m in each P616, P108, P117, P447, P511D, and P612
- 3 1.75oz/50g skeins of Koigu *Premium Merino* (100% wool), 175yd/161m in each 2170 and 2340
- Size US 3 (3.25mm) needles OR SIZE TO OBTAIN GAUGE
- Size D/3 (3mm) crochet hook, or size to correspond with needle
- 3 latch-style clasps

GAUGE

28 stitches and 36 rows = 4" (10cm) in stockinette stitch.
TAKE TIME TO CHECK GAUGE.

TECHNIQUES

See Stitch Workshop for:

- Practice square
- Joining seams with 2 needles and a crochet hook

SQUARE PATTERN

Refer to chart for colors used for each square. Cast on, or pick up and knit, 13 for a small square, 25 for a medium square, or 49 sts for a large square.

Row 1 (WS) Sl 1 p wise, k to last st, p1.
Row 2 Sl 1 purlwise, k to center 3 sts, SK2P, k to last st, p1.
Rep these 2 rows until you have 3 sts left.
If the chart indicates that the square is knitted using 2 colors (split square), begin with variegated color, and switch colors every RS row.
Next row K3tog.
Cut yarn, and slide tail through remaining loop.

JACKET

Create 4 sections as shown in chart, working squares in numerical order. Or, jacket can be made in one piece with no joining.
The green lines indicate the foundation row for each square. A solid green line means cast on sts, and a broken green line means pick up sts from adjacent squares as shown.
Pick up all sts with RS facing, rotating fabric as necessary.
Knit all sts in this garment through the back loop.

FINISHING

Join center back seam, top and bottom shoulder seams, and side seams with 2 needles and a crochet hook. The jagged edges of the panels should fit like a jigsaw puzzle.
Work 2 rows in sc around all edges using 2340. Sew clasps onto front panels starting at the top, and spacing them about 4"/10cm apart.

BLOCKING

Place jacket flat on a towel and pin to measurements, Spray with water and allow to dry. ◆

Left Back

Right Back

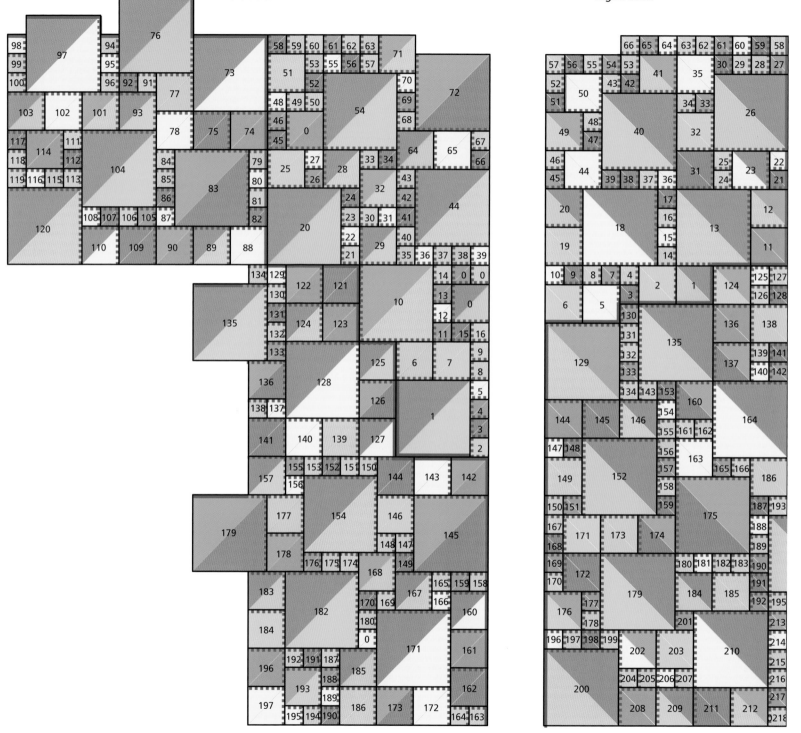

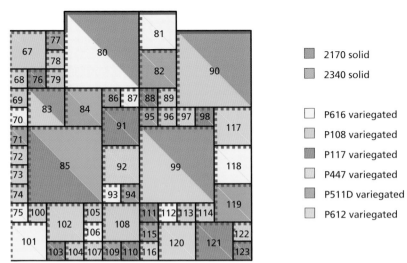

- [■] 2170 solid
- [■] 2340 solid

- [□] P616 variegated
- [□] P108 variegated
- [■] P117 variegated
- [□] P447 variegated
- [■] P511D variegated
- [□] P612 variegated

195

Right Front

Left Front

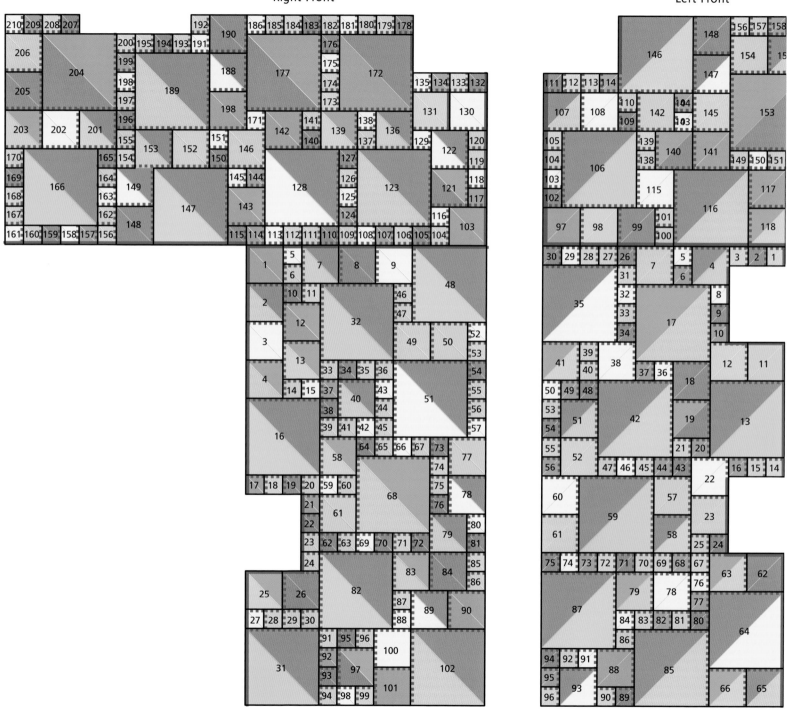

159 181 184 195 201
5 180 183 194 196 197 198 199 200
179 182 185 186 187 188 189 190 192 193
167 168 178
166 174 177 191
163 164 165 176
162 175
160 173
152 161 169 170 171 172 173
122 129 136
121 125 131 135 137
120 128
119 123 127 130 132 134
124 126 138

■ 2170 solid

■ 2340 solid

□ P616 variegated

□ P108 variegated

■ P117 variegated

□ P447 variegated

■ P511D variegated

□ P612 variegated

KNITTED MEASUREMENTS

◆ Bust 48"/122cm

◆ Length 27"/68cm

MATERIALS

◆ 19 1.75oz/50g skeins of Koigu *Painter's Palette Premium Merino* (100% wool), 175yd/161m in P155

◆ 1 1.75oz/50g skein of Koigu *Premium Merino* (100% wool), 175yds/161m in 2329

◆ Size US 3 (3.25mm) needles OR SIZE TO OBTAIN GAUGE

◆ Size D/3 (3mm) crochet hook, or size to correspond with needle

GAUGE

28 stitches and 36 rows = 4" (10cm) in stockinette stitch.

TAKE TIME TO CHECK GAUGE.

TECHNIQUES

See Stitch Workshop for:

◆ Practice square

◆ Triangles

◆ Joining seams with 2 needles and a crochet hook

Note Knit all sts in this garment through the back loop.

Mosaic Jacket (Adult)
intermediate

The Mosaic Jacket has a professional, tailored look. The mini-mitered design creates an appealing fabric, especially in the variegated yarn. This jacket makes a great take-along project. There is no breaking the yarn; just go from one square to the next, and the yarn makes the pattern.

SQUARE PATTERN

Cast on, or pick up and knit, 13 sts.

Row 1 (WS) Sl 1 p wise, k to last st, p1.

Row 2 Sl 1 p wise, k to center 3 sts, SK2P, k to last st, p1.

Rep these 2 rows until you have 3 sts left.

Next row SK2P.

Leave last loop on the needle.

RIGHT SLANT TRIANGLE PATTERN

Cast on, or pick up and knit, 7 sts.

Row 1 (WS) Knit.

Row 2 K to last 2 sts, k2tog.

Rep these 2 rows until you have 2 sts left.

Next row K2tog.

Leave last loop on the needle.

LEFT SLANT TRIANGLE PATTERN

Cast on, or pick up and knit, 7 sts.

Row 1 (WS) Knit.

Row 2 SKP, k to end.

Rep these 2 rows until you have 2 sts left.

Next row SKP.

Leave last loop on the needle

LEFT FRONT

Row 1 Begin at right edge. Cast on 13 sts, and work a square. With RS facing, pick up and knit 7 sts down left edge of square, then cast on 6 more sts (13 sts). Complete square. Work 13 additional squares the same way (15 squares).

Row 2 Begin at left edge. Cast on 6 sts, k7, then with WS facing, pick up and knit 6 sts across top edge of last square of previous row. Complete square. With WS facing, pick up and knit 7 sts down right edge of 1st square, and 6 more sts along top edge of next square of previous row. Complete square. Complete row in this manner (15 squares).

Row 3 Begin at right edge. Cast on 6 sts, k7, then with RS facing, pick up and knit 6 sts across top edge of last square of previous row. Complete square. With RS facing, pick up and knit 6 sts down left edge of 1st square, and 6 more sts along top edge of next square of previous row. Complete square. Complete row in this manner (15 squares).

Work 14 more rows in this manner (17 rows total).

Row 18 Begin at left edge. Work in pattern over 15 squares. With WS facing, pick up and knit 7 sts down right edge of last square, then cast on 6 sts. Complete square. Work 15 more squares in this manner (31 squares).

Rows 19–25 Work in pattern over 31 squares. Cut yarn, and slide tail through remaining loop.

Row 26 Begin at left edge. Skip first 4 squares. With new yarn and WS facing, pick up and knit 7 sts across top edge of 5th square. Work a right slant triangle. With WS facing, pick up and knit 7 sts down right edge of triangle, and 6 more sts across top edge of next square of previous row. Work 25 more squares in this manner (26 squares).

Rows 27–30 Work in pattern over 26 squares.

Row 31 Begin at right edge. Work in pattern over 26 squares. With RS facing, pick up and knit 7 sts down left edge of last square, and work a right slant triangle. Cut yarn, and slide tail through remaining loop.

RIGHT FRONT

Rows 1–17 Work same as left front, reversing all shaping to create a mirror image version of left front. Cut yarn, and slide tail through remaining loop.

Row 18 Begin at left edge. With new yarn, cast on 13 sts, and work a square. With WS facing, pick up and knit 6 sts down right edge of square, then cast on 6 sts. Work another square. Work 14 more squares in this manner (16 squares). With WS facing, pick up and knit 6 sts down right edge of last square, and 6 more across top edge of last square of previous row. Complete square. Work 14 more squares in this manner (31 squares).

Rows 19–25 Work in pattern over 31 squares.

Row 26 Begin at left edge. Work in pattern over 26 squares. With WS facing, pick up and knit 7 sts down right edge of last square. Work a right slant triangle, knitting the last st of every WS row together with a top edge st of next square of previous row. Cut yarn, and slide tail through remaining loop.

Row 27 Begin at right edge. Cast on 7 sts, then with RS facing, pick up and knit 6 sts across top edge of last square of previous row. Complete row in pattern (26 squares).

Rows 28–30 Work in pattern over 26 squares.

Row 31 Begin at right edge. Cast on 6 sts, and work a left slant triangle. Cut yarn, and slide tail through remaining loop. With new yarn and RS facing, pick up and knit 7 sts along cast on edge of triangle, and 6 more across top

edge of last square of previous row. Complete square. Complete row in pattern (26 squares).

BACK

Row 32 (this row connects the two pieces) Begin at left edge. Work 27 squares in pattern over right front, picking up for last square from triangle of previous row. With WS facing, pick up and knit 7 sts down right edge of last square, then cast on 6 sts. Complete square. Work 7 more squares in this manner (35 squares). With WS facing, pick up and knit 7 sts down right edge of last square, and 6 more across top edge of triangle from left front. Work 26 more squares in pattern (62 squares).

Rows 33–41 Work in pattern over 62 squares. Cut yarn, and slide tail through remaining loop.

Row 42 Begin at left edge. Skip 16 squares. With new yarn, cast on 6 sts, then with WS facing, pick up and knit 7 sts across top edge of 17th square. Work 29 more squares in pattern (30 squares).

Row 43–58 Work in pattern over 30 squares. Cut yarn, and slide tail through remaining loop.

FINISHING

Sew sleeve and side seams, leaving bottom 3 squares at each side open for side slits.

CROCHET EDGING

Outer edge

Work 1 row in sc using 2329.

Along front edges only: Work 1 more row in sc using 2329, and 1 more using P155.

Across bottom edge only Work 1 row in hdc using 2329.

Around neck edge only Work 1 row in dc using 2329, then work 2 rows in sc using P155.

Work next 2 rows using 2329.

Row 1 Work (dc, ch 2) into every other sc around.

Row 2 Work 3 sc into every sp around.

Sleeve cuffs

Work 1 row in sc, then 1 row in dc using 2329.

Work 2 rows in sc using P155.

Work next 2 rows using 2329.

Row 1 Work (dc, ch 2) into every other sc around.

Row 2 Work 3 sc into every ch-2 space around.

BLOCKING

Place jacket flat on a towel and pin to measurements. Spray with water and allow to dry. ◆

Mosaic Chart Adult

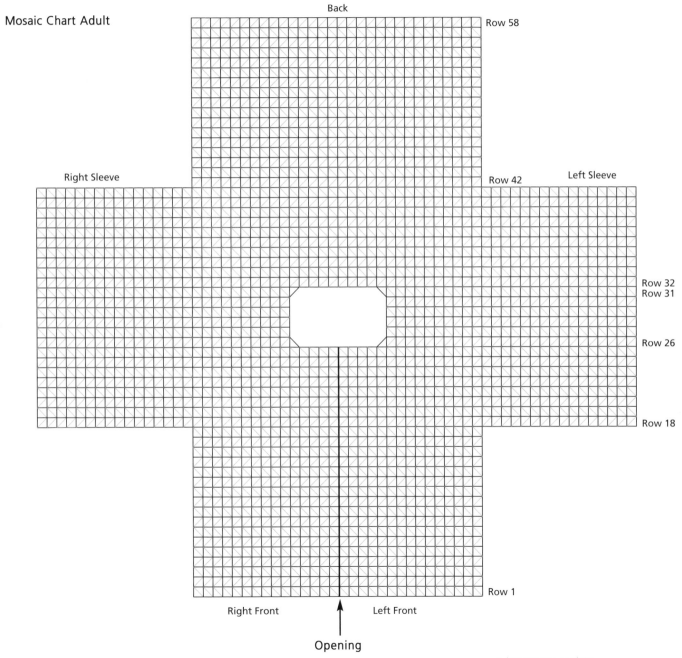

Back

Row 58

Right Sleeve

Row 42

Left Sleeve

Row 32
Row 31

Row 26

Row 18

Row 1

Right Front

Left Front

Opening

Mosaic Jacket (Child)
intermediate

KNITTED MEASUREMENTS

◆ Chest 32"/82cm

◆ Length 17"/44cm

MATERIALS

◆ 8 1.75oz/50g skeins of Koigu *Painter's Palette Premium Merino* (100% wool), 175yd/161m in P843

◆ 1 1.75oz/50g skein of Koigu *Premium Merino* (100% wool), 175yd/161m in 2170

◆ Size US 3 (3.25mm) needles OR SIZE TO OBTAIN GAUGE

◆ Size D/3 (3mm) crochet hook, or size to correspond with needle

GAUGE

28 stitches and 36 rows = 4" (10cm) in stockinette stitch.

TAKE TIME TO CHECK GAUGE.

Note Knit all sts in this garment through the back loop.

SQUARE PATTERN

Cast on, or pick up and knit, 13 sts.

Row 1 (WS) Sl 1 p wise, k to last st, p1.

Row 2 Sl 1 p wise, k to center 3 sts, SK2P, k to last st, p1.

Rep these 2 rows until you have 3 sts left.

Next row SK2P.

Leave last loop on the needle.

RIGHT SLANT TRIANGLE PATTERN

Cast on, or pick up and knit, 7 sts.

Row 1 (WS) Knit.

Row 2 K to last 2 sts, k2tog.

Rep these 2 rows until you have 2 sts left.

Next row K2tog.

Leave last loop on the needle.

LEFT SLANT TRIANGLE PATTERN

Cast on, or pick up and knit, 7 sts.

Row 1 (WS) Knit.

Row 2 SKP, k to end.

Rep these 2 rows until you have 2 sts left.

Next row SKP.

Leave last loop on the needle.

LEFT FRONT

Row 1 Begin at right edge. Cast on 13 sts, and work a square. With RS facing, pick up and knit 7 sts down left edge of square, then cast on 6 more sts (13 sts). Complete square. Work 9 additional squares the same way (11 squares).

Row 2 Begin at left edge. Cast on 6 sts, k7, then with WS facing, pick up and knit 6 sts across top edge of last square of previous row. Complete square. With WS facing, pick up and knit 6 sts down right edge of first square, and 6 more sts along top edge of next square of previous row. Complete square. Complete row in this manner (11 squares).

Row 3 Begin at right edge. Cast on 6 sts, k7, then with RS facing, pick up and knit 6 sts across top edge of last square of previous row.

Complete square. With RS facing, pick up and knit 7 sts down left edge of first square, and 6 more sts along top edge of next square of previous row. Complete square. Complete row in this manner (11 squares).

Work 10 more rows in this manner (13 rows total).

Row 14 Begin at left edge. Work in pattern across 11 squares. With WS facing, pick up and knit 7 sts down right edge of last square, and work a left slant triangle.

Row 15 Begin at right edge. Cast on 7 sts, and work a left slant triangle. Cut yarn, and slide tail through remaining loop. With new yarn and RS facing, pick up and knit 7 sts along cast on edge of triangle, and 6 more sts across top edge of triangle of previous row. Work 11 more squares in pattern (12 squares).

Row 16 Begin at left edge. Work 13 squares in pattern, picking up for last square from triangle of previous row. With WS facing, pick up and knit 7 sts down right edge of last square, then cast on 6 sts. Complete square. Work 13 more squares in this manner (27 squares).

Rows 17–20 Work evenly in pattern over 27 squares.

Row 21 Begin at right edge. Work 24 squares in pattern, omitting last 3 squares in the row.

Rows 22 and 23 Work in pattern over 24 squares. Cut yarn, and slide tail through remaining loop.

RIGHT FRONT

Rows 1–13 Work same as left front.

Row 14 Begin at left edge. Cast on 6 sts, and work a right slant triangle. Cut yarn, and slide tail through remaining loop. With new yarn and with WS facing, pick up and knit 7 sts along cast on edge of triangle, and 6 more sts across top edge of last square of row 13. Work 10 more squares in pattern (11 squares).

Row 15 Begin at right edge. Work 12 squares in pattern, picking up for last square from triangle of previous row. With RS facing, pick up and knit 6 sts down left edge of last square, and work a right slant triangle. Cut yarn, and slide tail through remaining loop.

Row 16 Begin at left edge. Cast on 13 sts, and complete a square. With WS facing, pick up and knit 6 sts down right edge of square, then cast on 6 sts. Complete another square. Work 12 more squares in this manner (14 squares). With WS facing, pick up and knit 6 sts down right edge of last square, and 6 more sts across top edge of triangle of previous row. Work to end of row in pattern (27 squares).

Rows 17–20 Work evenly in pattern over 27 squares. Cut yarn, and slide tail through remaining loop.

Row 21 Begin at right edge. Skip first 3 squares. With new yarn, cast on 7 sts, then with RS facing, pick up and knit 6 sts across top edge of 4th square. Work the rest of the row in pattern (24 squares).

Rows 22 and 23 Work in pattern over 24 squares.

BACK

Row 24 (this row connects the two pieces) Begin at left edge. Work in pattern over 24 squares of right front. With WS facing, pick up and knit 7 sts down right edge of last square, then cast on 7 sts. Complete square. Work 5 more squares in this manner (30 squares). With WS facing, pick up and knit 7 sts down right edge of last square, and 6 more across top edge of last square of left front. Work 23 more squares in pattern (54 squares).

Rows 25–29 Work in pattern over 54 squares. Cut yarn, and slide tail through remaining loop.

Row 30 Begin at left edge. Skip 14 squares. With new yarn and WS facing, pick up and knit 7 sts across top edge of 15th square. Work a right slant triangle. With WS facing, pick up and knit 7 sts down right edge of triangle, and 6 more across top edge of next square. Complete square. Work 23 more squares in this manner (24 squares). With WS facing, pick up and knit 7 sts down right edge of last square. Work a right slant triangle, knitting together the last st of every WS row with a top edge st of the next square. Cut yarn, and slide tail through remaining loop.

Row 31 Begin at right edge. With RS facing, pick up and knit 7 sts across top edge of last square of previous row. Work a left slant triangle. With RS facing, pick up and knit 7 sts down left edge of triangle, and 6 more across top edge of next square. Work 21 more squares in pattern (22 squares). With RS facing, pick up and knit 7 sts down left edge of last square. Work a left slant triangle, knitting the last st of every RS row together with a top edge at of next square. Cut yarn, and slide tail through remaining loop.

Row 32 Begin at left edge. With new yarn, cast on 7 sts, then pick up and knit 6 sts across top edge of last square of previous row. Work 21

more squares in pattern (22 squares).
Rows 33–44 Work evenly in pattern over 22
squares. Cut yarn, and slide tail through
remaining loop.

FINISHING
Sew sleeve and side seams, leaving bottom 2
squares at each side open.

CROCHET EDGING
With crochet hook and 2170 , work 1 row in sc
around outer edge, and around each sleeve.

Using P843, work around neck edge as follows:
*dc2tog into next sc, ch 1, skip 1 sc;
rep from * to end of neck, work evenly in sc
around remainder of outer edge.
Work 1 more row in sc using 2170 around
outer edge.

BLOCKING
Place jacket flat on a towel and pin to
measurements. Spray with water and allow
to dry. ◆

Mosaic Chart Child

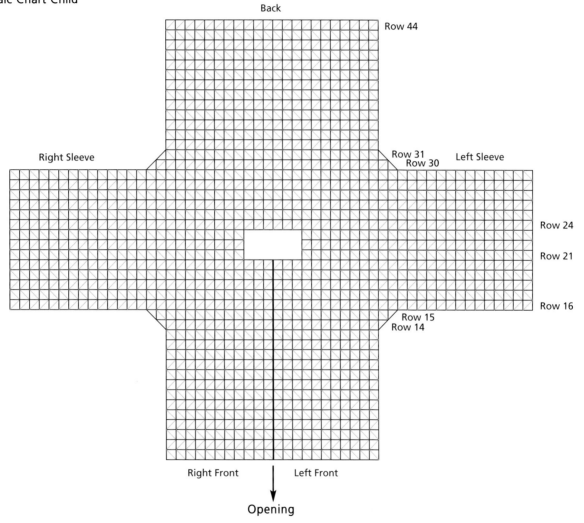

Back

Row 44

Right Sleeve

Row 31
Row 30

Left Sleeve

Row 24

Row 21

Row 16

Row 15
Row 14

Right Front

Left Front

Opening

KNITTED MEASUREMENTS

Pattern is given for Child's 4–6 yrs, 8–10 yrs, and 12–14 yrs, and adult small, medium, large, and extra large sizes.

◆ Chest/bust 27 (36, 36, 36, 42, 48, 56)"/68.5 (91.5, 91.5, 91.5, 106.5, 122, 142)cm

◆ Length 15 (17.5, 20, 24, 28, 24, 28)"/38 (44, 50, 60, 72, 60, 72)cm

MATERIALS

◆ 1 (1, 1, 1, 2, 2, 2) 1.75oz/50g skeins of Koigu *Painter's Palette Premium Merino* (100% wool), 175yd/161m in each P107, P419, P133, P116, P514, P126, P211, P426, P121, P127, P118

◆ Size US 3 (3.25mm) needles OR SIZE TO OBTAIN GAUGE

◆ Long circular needle in same size

◆ Set of 5 double pointed needles in same size.

◆ Size D/3 (3mm) crochet hook, or size to correspond with needle

GAUGE

28 stitches and 36 rows = 4" (10cm) in stockinette stitch.
TAKE TIME TO CHECK GAUGE.

TECHNIQUES

See Stitch Workshop for:

◆ Triangles

◆ Changing direction of decreases

◆ Joining seams with 2 needles and a crochet hook

Carousel Sweater

experienced

This tunic, composed of right-angle triangles knit together in modular knitting technique, incorporates eleven different variegated color combinations.

SQUARE PATTERN

Work each triangle in a different color of your choice, being sure that no two adjacent triangles are the same color.

Note: Weave in ends on WS as you work the triangles.

TRIANGLE 1

Cast on 11 (11, 11, 13, 15, 13, 15) sts using the knit cast on method.

Row 1 (WS) k to last st, p1

Row 2 Sl 1, k to last 3 sts, k2tog, p1.

Row 3 Sl 1, k to last st, p1.

Rep rows 2 and 3 until 2 sts rem.

Next row K2tog.

Cut yarn, and slide tail through remaining loop.

TRIANGLE 2

With RS facing, pick up 11 (11, 11, 13, 15, 13, 15) sts along right edge of triangle 1.

Work same as triangle 1.

Cut yarn, and slide tail through remaining loop.

TRIANGLE 3

With RS facing, pick up 11 (11, 11, 13, 15, 13, 15) sts along edge of triangle 1 (see carousel chart). Work as triangle 1.

TRIANGLE 4

With RS facing, pick up 11 (11, 11, 13, 15, 13, 15) sts along side of triangle 3 (see carousel chart).

Row 1 (WS) k10, k to last st, k last st tog with edge st of triangle 1.

Row 2 Sl 1 k to last 3 sts, k2tog, p1.

Row 3 Sl 1, k to last st, k last st tog with edge st of triangle 1.

Repeat rows 2 and 3 until 2 sts rem.

Next row k2tog.

Cut yarn, and slide tail through remaining loop.

FRONT and BACK

Make both pieces the same, using different color distributions. Begin all rows at right edge.

Row 1 Work bottom right square, following square pattern. Work 5 (7, 7, 5, 7, 5, 7) more squares, knitting the last st of every WS row of triangle 3 together with left edge st of previous square.

Row 2 Work a square, knitting the last st of every WS row of triangle 1 together with top edge st of first square of row 1. Work 5 (7, 7, 5, 7, 5, 7) more squares, joining them to each other same as row 1, and also joining them to previous row same as first square.

Work 2 (2, 3, 3, 2, 3, 2) more rows in this manner.

Next row (sleeves) Work 3 (3, 4, 4, 3, 4, 3) squares separately same as row 1, then work 6 (8, 8, 6, 8, 6, 8) squares, joining to top row of body, then work 3 (3, 4, 4, 3, 4, 3) more squares same as row 1, joining each only to previous square.

Work 0 (1, 1, 1, 2, 1, 2) more rows across 12 (14, 16, 14, 14, 14, 14) squares same as row 2.

Next row (neck) Work across 5 (6, 7, 6, 6, 6, 6)

squares in pattern, skip 2 square, then work across last 5 (6, 7, 6, 6, 6, 6) squares in pattern.

FINISHING

Join top and bottom sleeve seams and side seams with 2 needles and a crochet hook.

CROCHET EDGING

Child sizes Work 5 rows in sc around each edge in a dark variegated color of your choice.
Adult sizes Pick up and knit 160 (190, 160, 190) sts evenly around neck edge using double pointed needles. Work (4 rows St st, 4 rows reverse St st) twice, 4 rows St st, then 10 rows reverse St st. Fold last reverse St st inward, and sew to inside of edging.
Pick up and knit 250 (290, 335, 390) sts evenly around bottom edge of sweater using long circular needle. Work 4 rows st st, 4 rows reverse St st, 4 rows St st, then 10 rows reverse St st. Fold last reverse St st inward, and sew to inside of edging.
Pick up and knit 125 (145, 165, 195) sts evenly around each cuff using double pointed needles, and work edging same as bottom edge.

BLOCKING

Place sweater flat on a towel and pin to measurements. Spray with water and allow to dry. ◆

Carousel Chart

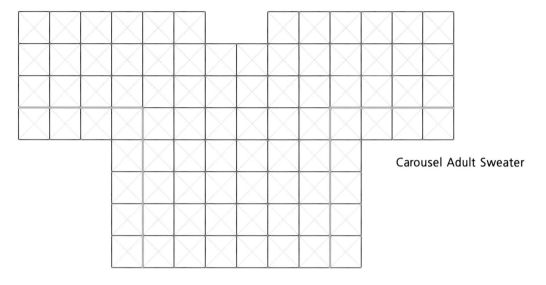

Carousel Adult Sweater

Small and large sizes—inside orange lines
Medium and extra large sizes—entire chart

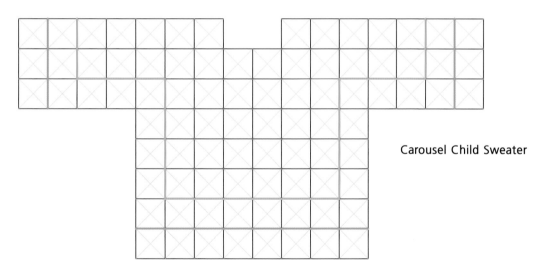

Carousel Child Sweater

Small—inside orange lines
Medium—inside green lines
Large—entire chart

KNITTED MEASUREMENTS

Pattern is given for small, medium, and large sizes.

◆ Bust 36 (41, 46)"/92 (104, 117)cm

◆ Length 16 (18, 20)"/40 (46, 50)cm

MATERIALS

◆ 2 1.75oz/50g skeins of Koigu *Painter's Palette Premium Merino* (100% wool), 175yd/161m in each P823D and P801B

◆ 1 1.75oz/50g skein of Koigu *Premium Merino* (100% wool), 175yd/161m in each 2180, 1260, 2220, and 2227

◆ Size US 3 (3.25mm) needles OR SIZE TO OBTAIN GAUGE

◆ Size D3 (3mm) crochet hook, or size to correspond with needle

GAUGE

28 stitches and 36 rows = 4" (10cm) in stockinette stitch.

TAKE TIME TO CHECK GAUGE.

TECHNIQUES

See Stitch Workshop for:

◆ Practice square

◆ Changing direction of decreases

Play Blocks Vest (Adult)
intermediate

Modular knitting requires short needles and little time to make each small square.
The Play Blocks Vest uses only one graph for three sizes. Increasing the size of the square changes the size of the finished garment.

LARGE SQUARE PATTERN

Cast on, or pick up and knit, 29 (33, 37) sts.

Row 1 WS Sl 1 p wise, k to last st, p1.

Row 2 Sl 1 p wise, k to center 3 sts, SK2P, k to last st, p1.

Rep these 2 rows until you have 3 sts left. If the chart indicates that the square is knitted using 2 colors, begin with variegated color, and switch colors every RS row.

Next row SK2P.

SMALL SQUARE PATTERN

Cast on, or pick up and knit, 15 (17, 19) sts, then work same as large square.

VEST

Row 1 Begin at right edge.

1st square Cast on 29 (33, 37) sts, and work a large square. Leave last loop on the needle.

2nd square With RS facing, pick up and knit 15 (17, 19) sts down left edge of first square, then cast on 14 (16, 18) more sts. Complete large square. Leave last loop on the needle. Work 7 more squares the same way. Fasten off.

10th square With WS facing, pick up and knit 15 (17, 19) sts up left edge of 9th square, then cast on 14 (16, 18) sts. Complete large square. Leave last loop on the needle.

Work 8 more squares the same way. Fasten off.

Row 2 Begin at left edge.

1st square Cast on 15 (17, 19) sts, and work a small square, knitting the last st of every WS row together with a top edge st of row 1. Leave last loop on the needle.

2nd square With RS facing, pick up and knit 8 (9, 10) sts up right edge of first square, then cast on 7 (8, 9) more sts. Complete small square, knitting the last st of every WS row together with a top edge st of row 1. Leave last loop on the needle. The bottom edges of 1st and 2nd squares should correspond with the top edge of the last square of row 1.

Work 16 more squares the same way. Cut yarn, and slide tail through remaining loop.

19th square With RS facing, pick up and knit 8 (9, 10) sts down right edge of 18th square, and 7 (8, 9) more sts across top edge of row 1. Complete small square. Leave last loop on the needle.

20th square With RS facing, pick up and knit 7 (8, 9) sts down right edge of 19th square, and 7 (8, 9) more sts across top edge of row 1.

Complete small square. Leave last loop on the needle. The bottom edges of 19th and 20th squares should correspond with the top edge of 9th square of row 1.

Work 16 more squares the same way. Fasten off.

Row 3 Begin at right edge.

1st square Cast on 15 (17, 19) sts, then with RS facing, pick up and knit 14 (18, 20) across top edges of last 2 squares of row 2. Complete large square. Leave last loop on the needle.

2nd square With RS facing, pick up and knit 15 (17, 19) sts down left edge of 1st square, and 14 (16, 18) more sts across top edges of next 2 small squares. Complete large square. Leave last loop on the needle.

Work 7 more squares the same way. Fasten off.

10th square With WS facing, pick up and knit 15 (17, 19) sts up left edge of 9th square, and 14 (16, 18) more sts across top edge of next 2 small squares. Complete large square knitting the last st of every RS row together with a top edge st of row 2. The bottom edge of this square should correspond with the top edges of the 8th & 9th squares of row 2.

Leave last loop on the needle.

11th square With WS facing, pick up and knit 15 (17, 19) sts up left edge of 10th square, and 14 (16, 18) more sts across top edge of next 2 small squares. Complete large square knitting the last st of every RS row together with a top edge st of row 2. Leave last loop on the needle. Work 7 more squares the same way. Fasten off.

Row 4 Work same as row 2.

Row 5 Work same as row 3.

Row 6 Begin at left edge

Left front Work same as left half of row 2 across first 4 large squares (make 8 small squares). Fasten off.

Back Work same as row 2 across center 8 large squares, changing direction of squares at center back (make 16 small squares). Fasten off.

Right Front Work same as right half of row 2 across last 4 large squares (make 8 small squares). Fasten off.

Row 7 Begin at right edge.

Right Front Work same as right half of row 3 across 8 small squares of right front (make 4

large squares). Fasten off.

Back Work same as row 3 across center 16 small squares, changing direction of squares at center back (make 8 large squares).

Left Front Work same as left half of row 3 across 8 small squares of left front (make 4 large squares). Fasten off.

Row 8 Work same as row 6.

Row 9 Begin at right edge.

Right Front Work same as right half of row 3 across left half of right front (make 2 large squares). Fasten off.

Back Work same as row 3 across center 16 small squares, changing direction of squares at center back (make 8 large squares).

Left Front Work same as left half of row 3 across right half of left front (make 2 large squares). Fasten off.

Row 10 Begin at left edge.

Left front shoulder Work same as left half of row 2 across 2 large squares of row 9 (make 4 small squares). Fasten off.

Left back shoulder Work 4 small squares same as left half of row 2 across 2 left large squares of back panel. Fasten off.

Right back shoulder Work 4 small squares same as right half of row 2 across 2 right large squares of back panel. Fasten off.

Right front shoulder Work same as right half of row 2 across 2 large squares of row 9 (make 4 small squares). Fasten off.

FINISHING

Join shoulder seams using 2 needles and a crochet hook.

Work a row in sc using color P823B around outer edge of vest, and around each armhole, then work another row using P801D.

BLOCKING

Place vest flat on a towel and pin to measurements. Spray with water and allow to dry. ◆

Play Blocks Chart Adult

Color Key

A- 2180   1 - P823D

B - 1260   2 - P801B

C - 2220

D - 2227

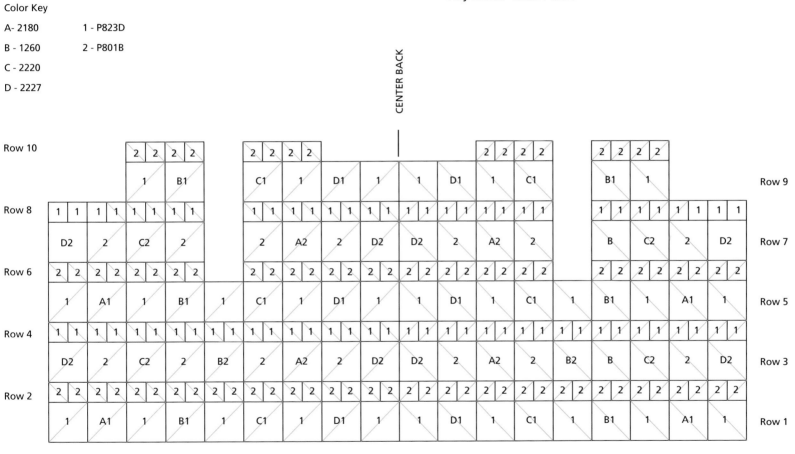

KNITTED MEASUREMENTS

Pattern is given for 2 yrs, 4 yrs, and 6–8 yrs.

◆ Chest 25 (27, 31)"/64 (68, 78)cm

◆ Length 10 (12, 13.5)"/25 (30, 34)cm

MATERIALS

◆ 1 1.75oz/50g skein of Koigu *Painter's Palette Premium Merino* (100% wool), 175yd/161m in each P106 and P123B

◆ 1 1.75oz/50g skein of Koigu *Premium Merino* (100% wool), 175yd/161m in each 2180, 2200, 2220, 2227, and 2130

◆ Size US 3 (3.25mm) needles OR SIZE TO OBTAIN GAUGE

◆ Size D/3 (3mm) crochet hook, or size to correspond with needle

GAUGE

28 stitches and 36 rows = 4" (10cm) in stockinette stitch.

TAKE TIME TO CHECK GAUGE.

TECHNIQUES

See Stitch Workshop for:

◆ Practice square

◆ Triangles

◆ Changing direction of decreases

Play Blocks Vest (Child)
intermediate

LARGE SQUARE PATTERN

Cast on, or pick up and knit, 19 (21, 25) sts.

Row 1 (WS) Sl 1 p wise, k to last st, p1.

Row 2 Sl 1 p wise, k to center 3 sts, SK2P, k to last st, p1.

Rep these 2 rows until you have 3 sts left. If the chart indicates that the square is knitted using 2 colors, begin with variegated color, and switch colors every RS row.

Next row SK2P.

SMALL SQUARE PATTERN

Cast on, or pick up and knit, 9 (11, 13) sts, then work same as large square.

LARGE RIGHT EDGE TRIANGLE PATTERN

Pick up and knit 10 (11, 13) sts.

Row 1 (WS) Sl 1, SKP, k to last st, p1.

Row 2 Sl 1, SKP, k to last st, p1.

Repeat these 2 rows until you have 2 sts left.

Next row K2tog.

SMALL RIGHT EDGE TRIANGLE PATTERN

Pick up and knit 5 (6, 7) sts, then work same as large right edge triangle.

LARGE LEFT EDGE TRIANGLE PATTERN

Pick up and knit 10 (11, 13) sts.

Row 1 (WS) Sl 1, Knit to last st , p1.

Row 2 Sl 1, k to last 3 sts, k2tog, p1.

Repeat these 2 rows until you have 2 sts left.

Next row K2tog.

SMALL LEFT EDGE TRIANGLE PATTERN

Pick up and knit 5 (6, 7) sts, then work same as large left edge triangle.

Row 1 Begin at right edge.

1st square Cast on 19 (21, 25) sts, and work a large square. Leave last loop on the needle.

2nd square With RS facing, pick up and knit 10 (11, 13) sts down left edge of 1st square, then cast on 9 (10, 12) more sts. Complete large square. Leave last loop on the needle.

Work 7 more squares the same way. Fasten off.

10th square With WS facing, pick up and knit 10 (11, 13) sts up left edge of 9th square, then cast on 9 (10, 12) sts. Complete large square. Leave last loop on the needle.

11th square With WS facing, pick up and knit 10 (11, 13) sts up left edge of 9th square, then cast on 9 (10, 12) sts. Complete large square. Leave last loop on the needle.

Work 7 more squares the same way. Fasten off.

Row 2 Begin at left edge.

1st square Cast on 9 (11, 13) sts, and work a small square, knitting the last st of every WS row together with a top edge st of row 1. Leave last loop on the needle.

2nd square With RS facing, pick up and knit 5 (6, 7) sts up right edge of 1st square, then cast on 4 (5, 6) more sts. Complete small square, knitting the last st of every WS row together with a top edge st of row 1. Leave last loop on the needle. The bottom edges of 1st and 2nd squares should correspond with the top edge of the last square of row 1.

Work 16 more squares the same way. Cut yarn, and slide tail through remaining loop.

19th square With RS facing, pick up and knit 5 (6, 7) sts down right edge of 18th square, and 4 (5, 6) more sts across top edge of row 1. Complete small square. Leave last loop on the needle.

20th square With RS facing, pick up and knit 5 (6,7) sts down right edge of 19th square, and 4 (5, 6) more sts across top edge of row 1. Complete small square. Leave last loop on the needle. The bottom edges of 19th and 20th squares should correspond with the top edge of 9th square of row 1.

Work 16 more squares the same way. Fasten off.

Row 3 Begin at right edge.

1st square Cast on 10 (11, 13) sts, then with RS facing, pick up and knit 9 (10, 12) across top edges of last 2 squares of row 2. Complete large square. Leave last loop on the needle.

2nd square With RS facing, pick up and knit 10 (11, 13) sts down left edge of 1st square, and 9 (10, 12) more sts across top edges of next 2 small squares. Complete large square. Leave last loop on the needle.

Work 7 more squares the same way. Fasten off.

10th square With WS facing, pick up and knit 10 (11, 13) sts up left edge of 9th square, and 9 (10, 12) more sts across top edge of next 2 small squares. Complete large square knitting the last st of every RS row together with a top edge st of row 2. The bottom edge of this square should correspond with the top edges of the 8th & 9th squares of row 2. Leave last loop on the needle.

11th square With WS facing, pick up and knit 10 (11, 13) sts up left edge of 10th square, and 9 (10, 12) more sts across top edge of next 2 small squares. Complete large square knitting the last st of every RS row together with a top edge st of row 2. Leave last loop on the needle.

Work 7 more squares the same way. Fasten off.

Row 4 Work same as row 2.

Row 5 Work same as row 3.

Row 6 Begin at left edge

Left front Work same as left half of row 2 across first 4 large squares (make 8 small squares). Fasten off. Skip 1 large square for armhole.

Back Work same as row 2 across center 8 large squares, changing direction of squares at center back (make 16 small squares). Fasten off. Skip 1 large square for armhole.

Right Front Work same as right half of row 2 across last 4 large squares (make 8 small squares). Fasten off.

Row 7 Begin at right edge.

Right Front With RS facing, pick up and knit 10 (11, 13) sts across last 2 small squares of row 6. Complete large right edge triangle. Leave last loop on the needle. Work next 3 squares same as right half of row 3. Fasten off.

Back Work same as row 3 across center 16 small squares, changing direction of squares at center back (make 8 large squares).

Left front Work 3 squares same as left half of row 3 across 6 small squares of left front.

Fasten off.

Pick up and knit 10 (11, 13) sts across last 2 small squares of left front. Complete large left edge triangle. Fasten off.

Row 8 Begin at left edge.

Left Front With RS facing, pick up and knit 5 (6, 7) across left half of last large square in row 7. Complete small left edge triangle. Fasten off. Work 5 more small squares same as left half of row 2 across remaining 2.5 large squares of left front. Fasten off.

Back Work same as row 2 across center 8 large squares, changing direction of squares at center back (make 16 small squares). Fasten off.

Right Front Work 5 squares same as right half of row 2 across 2.5 large squares of right front. Fasten off.

With RS facing, pick up and knit 5 (6, 7) sts across right half of first large square of row 7. Complete small right edge triangle. Fasten off.

Row 9 Begin at right edge.

Right front With RS facing, pick up and knit 5 (6, 7) sts across last small square of row 8. Complete small right edge triangle. Fasten off. Cast on 5 (6, 7) sts, then with RS facing, pick up and knit 5 (5, 6) sts down left edge of small triangle, and 9 (10, 12) more sts across top edges of next 2 small squares. Complete large square. Leave last loop on the needle.

Work 1 more large square same as right half of row 3 across top edges of last 2 small squares of right front. Fasten off.

Back Work same as row 3 across center 16 small squares, changing direction of squares at center back (make 8 large squares).

Left Front Work same as left half of row 3 across 4 small squares of left front (make 2 large squares). Leave last loop on the needle.

With RS facing, pick up and knit 5 (6, 7) sts across last small square of row 8. Complete small left edge triangle. Fasten off.

Row 10 Begin at left edge.

Left front shoulder Work same as left half of
row 2 across 2 large squares of row 9 (make 4
small squares). Fasten off.

Left back shoulder Work 4 small squares same
as left half of row 2 across 2 left large squares
of back panel. Fasten off.

Right back shoulder Work 4 small squares same
as right half of row 2 across 2 right large
squares of back panel. Fasten off.

Right front shoulder Work same as right half of
row 2 across 2 large squares of row 9 (make 4
small squares). Fasten off.

FINISHING

Join shoulder seams with 2 needles and a
crochet hook.

Work 2 rows in sc using color 2130 around
outer edge of vest, and around each armhole.

BLOCKING

Place vest flat on a towel and pin to
measurements. Spray with water and allow
to dry. ◆

Play Blocks Chart Child

Color Key

A - 2180   1 - P106

B - 2200   2 - P123B

C - 2220

D - 2227

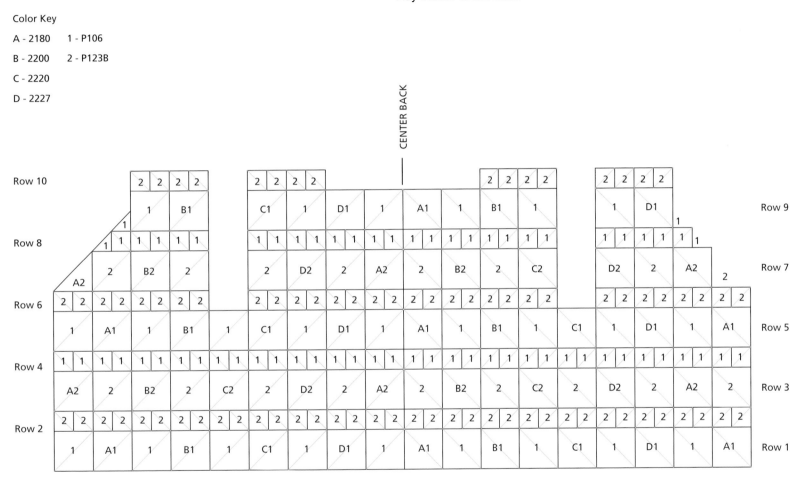

Jigsaw Vest
intermediate

This vest is for knitters who enjoy jigsaw puzzles. A genuine brain exercise, the pattern is not for beginners: It is absolutely essential to do a practice piece to learn the technique and the sizing of the squares. Once mastered, the technique is endlessly fascinating.

KNITTED MEASUREMENTS
- Bust 40 (44, 48)"/102 (112, 122)cm

MATERIALS
- 2 1.75oz/50g skeins of Koigu *Painter's Palette Premium Merino* (100% wool), 175yd/161m in each P134 and P706
- 2 1.75oz/50g skeins of Koigu *Premium Merino* (100% wool, solid color), 175yd/161m in 2340
- 1 1.75oz/50g skein of Koigu *Premium Merino* in each 2174, 1128, 1230, 2239, and 2166
- Size US 3 (3.25mm) needles OR SIZE TO OBTAIN GAUGE
- Size D/3 (3mm) crochet hook, or size to correspond with needle
- ⅛" leather cord about 40"/100cm in length
- 8 buttons ⅝" in diameter

GAUGE
28 stitches and 36 rows = 4" (10cm) in stockinette stitch.
TAKE TIME TO CHECK GAUGE.

TECHNIQUES
See Stitch Workshop for:
- Practice square
- Changing direction of decreases

SQUARE PATTERN
Knit all sts in this garment through the back loop.
Work colors according to chart.
Cast on or pick up and knit 39 (41, 43) sts.
Row 1 (WS) Sl 1 p wise, k to last st, p1.
Row 2 Sl 1 p wise, k to center 3 sts, SK2P, k to last st, p1.
Rep these 2 rows until you have 21 sts, then switch colors.
Continue as established until you have 3 sts left.
Next row SK2P.
Cut yarn, and slide tail through remaining loop.

PANEL A
Begin at top.
Top square
Cast on 39 (41, 43) sts, and complete square.
2nd square
With RS facing, pick up and knit 20 (21, 22) sts along bottom edge of top square. Cast on 19 (20, 21) more sts, and complete square.
Continue in this manner until you have 9 squares in panel A.

PANELS B & C
(work simultaneously)
Begin at bottom.

Bottom square of panel B
With RS facing, pick up and knit 20 (21, 22) sts down left edge of bottom square of panel A. Cast on 19 (20, 21) more sts, and complete square. Leave last loop on the needle.
Bottom square of panel C
With RS facing, pick up and knit 20 (21, 22) down left edge of bottom square of panel B. cast on 19 (20, 21) more sts, and complete square.
2nd square of panel B
With RS facing, pick up and knit 20 (21, 22) down left edge of second square of panel A, and 19 (20, 21) more sts along top edge of bottom square of panel B. Complete square. Leave last loop on the needle.
2nd square of panel C
With RS facing, pick up and knit 20 (21, 22) sts down left edge of second square of panel B, and 19 (20, 21) more sts along top edge of bottom square of panel C. Complete square. Continue in this manner until you have 9 squares in each panel B & C.
10th square of panel B
Cast on 20 (21, 22) sts. With RS facing, pick up and knit 19 (20, 21) more sts along top edge of 9th square of panel B. Complete square. Leave last loop on the needle.

10th square of panel C

With RS facing, pick up and knit 20 (21, 22) sts down left edge of 10th square of panel B, and 19 (20, 21) more sts along top edge of 9th square of panel C. Complete square.

Work 11th square of both panels the same way.

PANEL D

Begin at bottom.

Bottom square

With RS facing pick up and knit 20 (21, 22) sts down left edge of bottom square of panel C. Cast on 19 (20, 21) more sts, and complete square.

2nd Square

With RS facing pick up and knit 20 (21, 22) sts down left edge of 2nd square of panel C, and 19 (20, 21) more sts along top edge of bottom square of panel D. Complete square.

Continue in this manner until you have 7 squares in panel D.

PANEL E

Begin at bottom.

Bottom square Cast on 39 (41, 43) sts and complete square.

2nd square

With RS facing, pick up and knit 20 (21, 22) sts along top edge of bottom square. Cast on 19 (20, 21) more sts, and complete square.

Work 2 more squares the same way (4 squares).

5th square

Work as previous squares, knitting the last st of every WS row together with corresponding edge st of 5th square of panel D.

Work 2 more squares the same way, attaching to panel D on WS rows (7 squares).

PANELS F and G

(work simultaneously)

Begin at top.

Top square of panel G

Cast on 39 (41, 43) sts, and complete square. Leave last loop on the needle.

Top square of panel F

With RS facing, pick up and knit 20 (21, 22) sts up right edge of top square of panel G. Cast on 19 (20, 21) more sts, and complete square.

2nd square of panel G

Cast on 20 (21, 22) sts. With RS facing, pick up and knit 19 (20, 21) sts along bottom edge of top square of Panel F. Complete Square. Leave last loop on the needle.

2nd square of panel F

With RS facing, pick up and knit 20 (21, 22) sts up right edge of 2nd square of panel G, and 19 (20, 21) more sts along bottom edge of top square of panel F. Complete square.

Continue in this manner until you have 4 squares in each panel F and G.

5th square of panel G

Cast on 20 (21, 22) sts. With RS facing, pick up and knit 20 (21, 22) sts along bottom edge of 4th square of panel G Complete square. Leave last loop on the needle.

5th Square of panel F

Pick up and knit 20 (21, 22) sts up right edge of 5th square of panel G, and 19 (20, 21) more sts along bottom edge of 4th square of panel F. Complete square, knitting the last st of every RS row together with corresponding edge st of top square of panel E.

Continue in this manner, attaching to panel E on RS rows, until you have 11 squares in each panel F and G.

PANELS H and I
(work simultaneously)
Begin at bottom.
Bottom square of panel I
Cast on 39 (41, 43) sts, and complete square. Leave last loop on the needle.
Bottom square of panel H
With WS facing, pick up and knit 20 (21, 22) sts down right edge of bottom square of panel I. Cast on 19 (20, 21) more sts, and work square starting with row 2, and knitting the last st of every WS row together with corresponding edge st of bottom square of panel G.
2nd square of panel I
With RS facing, pick up and knit 20 (21, 22) sts along top edge of bottom square of panel I. Cast on 19 (20, 21) more sts, and complete square. Leave last loop on the needle.
2nd square of panel H
With WS facing, pick up and knit 20 (21, 22) sts

down right edge of 2nd square of panel I, and 19 (20, 21) more sts along top edge of bottom square of panel H. Work square starting with row 2, and knitting together the last st of every WS row with corresponding edge st of 2nd square of panel G.
Continue in this manner until you have 10 squares in each panel H and I.

PANELS J and K
(work simultaneously)
Work same as panels B and C.

PANEL L
Begin at top.
Top square
Cast on 20 (21, 22) sts. With RS facing, pick up and knit 19 (20, 21) more sts along left edge of 5th square (from top) of panel K. Complete square.
2nd square
With RS facing, pick up and knit 20 (21, 22) sts along bottom edge of top square, and 19 (20, 21) more sts down left edge of 6th square

(from top) of panel K.
Continue in this manner until you have 7 squares in panel L.

PANEL M
Begin at top.
Top square
Cast on 39 (41, 43) sts. Complete square, knitting together the last st of every RS row with corresponding edge st of top square of panel L.
2nd square
Cast on 20 (21, 22) sts. With RS facing, pick up and knit 19 (20, 21) more sts along bottom edge of top square. Complete square, knitting together the last st of every RS row with corresponding edge st of 2nd square of panel L. Make 1 more square in this manner, then make 4 more squares without attaching to panel L (7 squares).

PANELS N and O
(work simultaneously)
Work same as panels F and G.

PANEL P

Begin at top.

Top square

Cast on 20 (21, 22) sts. With RS facing, pick up and knit 19 (20, 21) more sts along left edge of 3rd square (from top) of panel O.
Complete square.

2nd square

With RS facing, pick up and knit 20 (21, 22) sts along bottom edge of top square, and 19 (20, 21) more sts down left edge of 4th square (from top) of panel O.

Continue in this manner until you have 9 squares in panel P.

FINISHING

Join shoulder seams with 2 needles and a crochet hook.

Work a row in sc around outer edge of vest, including slits and around each armhole using 2174. Work another row using P134, then another using 2174 again.

Sew 4 pairs of buttons across from each other at top 4 squares of front edges.

Cut leather cord into 4 equal lengths. Tie each into a figure 8, and secure around a pair of buttons to serve as a buttonhole.

BLOCKING

Place vest flat on a towel and pin to measurements. Spray with water and allow to dry. ◆

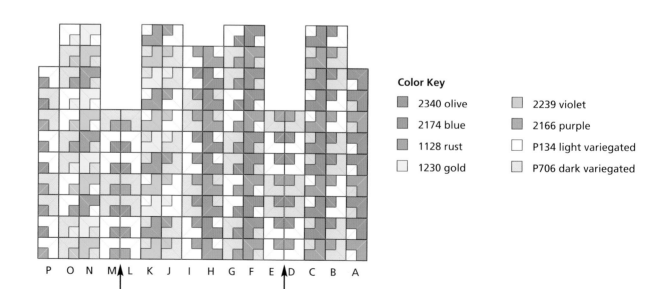

P   O   N   M   L   K   J   I   H   G   F   E   D   C   B   A

slit   slit

Color Key

■	2340 olive	■	2239 violet
■	2174 blue	■	2166 purple
■	1128 rust	□	P134 light variegated
□	1230 gold	■	P706 dark variegated

FINISHED MEASUREMENTS

Pattern is given for medium and large sizes.

◆ Bust 40 (44)"/102 (112)cm

◆ Length 20 (22)"/51 (56)cm

MATERIALS

◆ 2 1.75oz/50g skeins of Koigu *Painter's Palette Premium Merino* (100% wool), 175yd/161m in each of 3 variegated colors of your choice (6 skeins in total)

◆ 3 1.75oz/50g skeins of Koigu *Premium Merino* (100% wool), 175yd/161m a dark solid color, and 3 skeins in a light solid color of your choice (6 skeins in total).

◆ Size US 3 (3.25mm) needles OR SIZE TO OBTAIN GAUGE

◆ Size D/3 (3mm) crochet hook, or size to correspond with needle

◆ 3 (4) latch-style clasps

GAUGE

28 stitches and 36 rows = 4" (10cm) in stockinette stitch.

TAKE TIME TO CHECK GAUGE.

Refer to charts for colors used.

TECHNIQUES

See Stitch Workshop for:

◆ Practice square

◆ Changing direction of decreases

◆ Joining seams with 2 needles and a crochet hook

Log Cabin Vest
intermediate

This semi-fitted short vest is composed of many squares knit in garter stitch with random color distribution. The squares can be joined together either horizontally or vertically. This pattern calls for two solid colors, with different variegates, used interchangeably.

SQUARE PATTERN

Cast on, or pick up and knit, 25 sts.

Row 1 (WS) Sl 1 p wise, k to last st, p1.

Row 2 Sl 1 p wise, k to center 3 sts, SK2P, k to last st, p1.

Rep these 2 rows until you have 3 sts left. If the chart indicates that the square is knitted using 2 colors, begin with variegated color, and switch colors every RS row.

Next row SK2P.

Cut yarn, and slide tail through remaining loop.

RIGHT HALF

Begin all rows at right edge.

Row 1

1st square Cast on 25 sts, and work a square.

2nd square With RS facing, pick up and knit 13 sts down left edge of first square, then cast on 12 more sts. Complete square.

Work 8 (9) more squares the same way.

Row 2

1st square Cast on 13 sts, then with RS facing, pick up and knit 12 sts across top edge of 1st square of row 1. Complete square.

2nd square With RS facing, pick up and knit 13 sts down left edge of 1st square, then pick up and knit 12 sts across top of next square of row 1. Complete square.

Work 8 (9) more squares the same way.

Rows 3–5 Work same as row 2.

MEDIUM SIZE ONLY

Rows 6 and 7 Work across first 4 squares, skip 2 center squares, then work across last 4 squares.

Rows 8 and 9 Skip 1st & 2nd squares, work across 2 last squares of right front, then work across all 4 squares of right back.

Row 10 (shoulders) Work across 2 squares of right front, then across 1st and 2nd squares only of right back.

LARGE SIZE ONLY

Rows 6–8 Work across first 5 squares, skip 1 square, then work across last 5 squares.

Rows 9 and 10 Skip 1st and 2nd squares, work across last 3 squares of right front, then work across all 5 squares of right back.

Row 11 (shoulders) Work across 3 squares of right front, then across first 3 squares only of right back.

LEFT HALF

Begin all rows at left edge.

Row 1

1st square Cast on 25 sts, and work a square.

2nd square With WS facing, pick up and knit 13 sts down right edge of first square, then cast on 12 more sts. Complete square.

Work 8 (9) more squares the same way.

Row 2

1st square Cast on 13 sts, then with WS facing, pick up and knit 12 sts across top edge of first square of row 1. Complete square.

2nd square With WS facing, pick up and knit 13 sts down right edge of first square, then pick up and knit 12 sts across top of next square of row 1. Complete square.

Work 8 (9) more squares the same way.

Rows 3–5 Work same as row 2.

MEDIUM SIZE ONLY

Rows 6 and 7 Work across first 4 squares, skip 2

center squares, then work across last 4 squares.

Rows 8 and 9 Skip 1st and 2nd square, work across 2 last squares of left front, then work across all 4 squares of left back.

Row 10 (shoulders) Work across 2 squares of left front, then across 1st and 2nd squares only of left back.

LARGE SIZE ONLY

Rows 6–8 Work across first 5 squares, skip 1 square, then work across last 5 squares.

Rows 9 and 10 Skip 1st and 2nd squares, work across last 3 squares of left front, then work across all 5 squares of left back.

Row 11 (shoulders) Work across 3 squares of left front, then across first 3 squares only of left back.

FINISHING

Sew shoulder seams and center back seam.

Work 4 rows in sc using 4 different colors of your choice around outer edge of vest, and around each armhole.

Sew buttons onto front pieces, approximately 4"/10cm apart.

BLOCKING

Place vest flat on a towel and pin to measurements. Spray with water and allow to dry. ◆

Log Cabin Chart Large

Color Key
A - Light solid KPM
B - Dark solid KPM

1 - 1st variegated KPPPM
2 - 2nd variegated KPPPM
3 - 3rd variegated KPPPM

Left Half (Left front | Left back)

Row	Left front					Left back				
Row 11	B2	1	A3			3	B3	A1		
Row 10	A3	B2	A1			A2	2	B2	A3	3
Row 9		3	A3	B1		1	B1	A2	2	B1
Row 8	A1	1	B1	B3	A3	B2	A1	3	B2	A2
Row 7	2	B2	2	A2	1	A2	2	B2	A1	2
Row 6	B3	B1	A1	1	B3	B2	B3	A3	3	B1
Row 5	A2	A3	3	B2	A1	B3	2	A2	3	B3	A2	3
Row 4	B2	2	B3	A3	B1	3	A1	2	B2	A3	3
Row 3	3	1	A2	3	2	A2	B3	B2	A2	B1	B3
Row 2	B1	A1	2	1	A3	B1	3	A1	B2	1	3
Row 1	A3	3	B2	A1	B1	1	A2	B2	2	B3	B2

Right Half (Right back | Right front)

Row	Right back					Right front				
Row 11	A3	B1	3			B2	1	A3		
Row 10	B2	A2	B1	1	B3	2	B2	2		
Row 9	A1	B2	A3	A2	1	A3	3	B1		
Row 8	3	B1	A1	3	B2	B2	A1	B3	A1	1
Row 7	B3	2	B2	A2	B3	3	B2	A2	2	B3
Row 6	A1	B2	2	B1	A3	A1	3	B3	A3	2
Row 5	1	A3	B2	B3	1	A3	2	B2	A1	1	B1
Row 4	B1	2	A1	B1	B2	1	A3	3	B2	A2	2
Row 3	2	B2	2	A2	3	B1	B2	A1	3	B3	A3
Row 2	B3	B1	1	B3	A3	B2	2	B2	A3	2	B1
Row 1	1	A3	3	B1	1	A1	B2	3	B1	A3	1

(Center Back divides Left Half and Right Half)

Log Cabin Chart Medium

Color Key
A - Light solid KPM
B - Dark solid KPM

1 - 1st variegated KPPPM
2 - 2nd variegated KPPPM
3 - 3rd variegated KPPPM

Left Half (Left front | Left back)

Row	Left front					Left back				
Row 10	B2	A1				A2	2			
Row 9	A3	B1				1	B1	A3	2	
Row 8	B3	3				B2	A1	3	B2	
Row 7	A1	B2	2	A2		A2	2	B2	A1	
Row 6	2	B1	A1	1		B2	B3	A3	3	
Row 5	B3	A3	3	B2	A1	B2	2	A2	3	B3
Row 4	A2	B2	B3	A3	B1	3	A1	2	B2	A3
Row 3	B2	1	A2	3	2	A2	B3	B2	A2	B1
Row 2	3	A1	2	1	A3	B1	3	A1	B2	1
Row 1	A3	3	B2	A1	B1	1	A2	B2	2	B3

Right Half (Right back | Right front)

Row	Right back					Right front				
Row 10	1	B3				2	B2			
Row 9	B3	1	A2	1		A3	3			
Row 8	B1	A1	3	B2		B2	A1			
Row 7	2	B2	A2	B3		3	B2	A2	2	
Row 6	B2	2	B1	A3		A1	3	B3	A3	
Row 5	A3	B2	B3	1	A2	2	B2	A1	1	B1
Row 4	1	A1	B1	B2	1	A3	3	B2	A2	2
Row 3	B2	2	A2	3	B1	B2	A1	3	B3	A3
Row 2	B1	1	B3	A3	B2	2	B2	A3	2	B1
Row 1	A3	3	1	B1	A1	B2	3	B1	A1	1

(Center Back divides Left Half and Right Half)

Abbreviations

ch	chain
cm	centimeter
dc	double crochet
dec	decrease
foll	follow(s)(ing)
g	gram
i-cord	knitted cord
k	knit
k wise	knitwise. Insert the needle as if to knit.
k2tog	knit two stitches together. One stitch has been decreased.
K3tog	knit three stitches together. Two stitches have been decreased.
LH	left hand
m	meter
mm	millimeter
m1	make one
oz	ounce
p	purl
pat	pattern
pick up	Insert RH needle into stitch p wise and transfer without knitting.

p wise	purlwise. Insert the needle as if to purl
p2sso	pass two slip stitches over
rem	remain(ing)
rnd(s)	rounds
rep(s)	repeat(s)
rev	revise
RH	right hand
RS	right side
sc	single crochet
SKP	slip 1, knit 1, pass slip stitch over. One stitch has been decreased.
SK2P	slip 1, knit 2 together, pass slip stitch over the knit 2 together. Two stitches have been decreased.
sl	slip
st(s)	stitch(es)
St st	stockinette stitch
tbl	through back loop
tog	together
WS	wrong side
yo	yarn over needle

Acknowledgments

A great many friends and family have helped and supported the Koigu journey. We are very grateful for their wisdom, helpful hands, guidance and inspiration, and for sometimes just lending a friendly ear.

Thank you to the following people who made this book possible: Trisha Malcolm, Elaine Silverstein, Chi Ling Moy, Erica Smith, Sheena T. Paul, Erin Walsh, Carla Scott, Rosemary Drysdale, Shiri Mor, Shirley Scott, Mary Lou Eastman, David Joinnides, Mooishi, Dan Howell and Art Joinnides.

To all the stores that make Koigu yarn and patterns available to the knitting world, thank you.

To the Koigu ambassadors, knitters who have been there encouraging and supporting us from the beginning, thank you for your support.

Many many thanks to my daughter and business partner, Taiu. Her endless patience, perseverance and good humor have made this book possible and brought our business where it is today.

Further Readings

Fassett, Kaffe, *Glorious Knitting*.
London: Century Publishing, 1985.

Luters, Ginger, Module Magic:
Creative Projects to Knit 1 Block at a Time.
Sioux Falls, South Dakota: XRX Books, 2004.

Potter, Cheryl, and Alexis Yiorgos Xenakis.
Handpaint Country: A Knitter's Journey.
Sioux Falls, South Dakota: XRX Books, 2002.

Schulz, Horst, *Patchwork Knitting*:
Pullovers, Jackets, Waistcoats.
East London, South Africa:
Saprotex International, 2000.

Skolnik, Linda, and Janice MacDaniels.
The Knitting Way. Woodstock, Vermont:
Skylight Paths Publishing, 2005.

Xenakis, Alexis Yiorgos.
"The Knitters Next Door."
Knitters Magazine, 14:4 (Winter 1997).

Zelanski, Paul, and Mary Pat Fisher.
Color.
3rd ed. Prentice Hall, 1999.

Resources

For a list of select shops in the United States, Canada and overseas, please write to the address below or visit our Web site.

KOIGU WOOL DESIGNS

Box 158

563295 Glenelg Holland Townline

Chatsworth, ON N0H1G0

1-888-765-WOOL

519-794-3066

Fax 519-794-3130

www.koigu.com